# THE *Psychology* OF
# EVERYDAY LIVING

BY

ERNEST DICHTER

*Consulting Psychologist*

BARNES & NOBLE, INC.

*New York*

MANUFACTURED IN THE UNITED STATES OF AMERICA

# ACKNOWLEDGMENTS

Many people coöperated in the preparation of this book. The author is particularly grateful to more than ten thousand individuals who patiently submitted to long interviews and provided essential information.

The data in certain chapters were assembled under the auspices of J. Stirling Getchell Company, the Columbia Broadcasting System, Inc., and the Crowell-Collier Publishing Company. Some of the discussions in Part I (Successful Living—Attitudes and Emotions) are based on articles written by the author for *Look* magazine, in which they were printed under the headings "Psychoquiz" and "Personality Clinic." The section on the psychology of smoking is an elaboration of an article prepared by the author for *Coronet* magazine. Part IV is based largely on brief articles prepared for the *Journal of Living*. The sections "Are You Fit to Be Your Own Boss?" and "How to Feel Good at the End of a Day" were written originally for *Pageant* magazine. The section "Fool Yourself and Like It" appeared in *Your Life* magazine.

The author is most indebted to Dr. Samuel Smith, of Barnes and Noble Company, who rearranged and edited the material; to Virginia Forsythe, Associate Editor of *Look* magazine; to Leonard M. Leonard, Editor of the *Journal of Living;* to William E. Berchtold, formerly with J. Stirling Getchell Company; and to Dr. Virginia Miles and Jeannette Green for invaluable assistance in field studies and research. Dr. Leo Winter, psychologist, drew the cartoons for the book.

ERNEST DICHTER

# INTRODUCTION

True happiness depends largely on the little things of life —what we eat, the clothes we wear, our everyday activities. Ideals and lofty ambitions, love and beauty, are fine visions, but they have to be translated into terms of daily living. This book endeavors to show how familiar habits and minor enjoyments are linked inseparably to the ideal of "life, liberty, and the pursuit of happiness."

The skilled advertiser tries to sell his merchandise by associating it with ideas of success, security, and social prestige. These are the same things which statesmen and educators strive to help us to achieve. To succeed, both the advertiser and the teacher should appeal to us in the same way —by "selling" us the means of happiness, that is, ways of living that will bring success, security, and social prestige. In our pursuit of happiness, we cannot rely on ideals alone; we have to get down to earth. When we enjoy our coffee or "coke" in the morning, that's part of happiness. A good night's sleep is part of happiness. Seeing an exciting "movie" about scientific achievements and imagining that we, too, could become great inventors—this, also, is part of happiness.

An understanding of life is the basis for enjoyable living. So let us ask a few questions that will test our understanding. Why do we usually eat the same kind of breakfast every morning? Why do we raise our hats when greeting a friend? Why do we use soap? The answers to even such apparently inconsequential questions about our daily habits will help to disclose how rich in happiness our lives can be. That is, the answers will help, if only we understand ourselves and reshape our actions accordingly.

*Life is a psychological problem.* Each day brings new tasks which life poses in the course of its normally even development. These tasks may concern ourselves only, or their performance may influence other people directly. In either case, the successful solution of a problem will depend upon how well its psychological aspect has been handled. To acquire efficiency in our occupation, in our daily tasks, we must be able to control our emotions, master human relations, and apply important psychological principles. For instance, to advertise merchandise effectively, we must be familiar with the emotions and the motives of people. In the same way, success in the political affairs of a democracy requires the ability to coöperate with others and to think independently.

In other words, all of us have to apply sound psychology continuously if we are to succeed in whatever we are doing. We need, therefore, to explore those scientific truths about everyday life that will help anyone to live more efficiently and deal more successfully with other people. In this book we do not propose to discuss technical psychological laboratory experiments, but rather to analyze in an interesting way our everyday living: the things we do during our waking hours to express our true personalities. In this case, therefore, our laboratory is life itself, and our approach to the study of human behavior should be far more useful, as well as far more interesting, than detailed descriptions of experiments on the neuroses of rats. This study of psychological principles will deal, as it should, with the everyday problems that confront us as individual consumers, advertisers, educators—average citizens.

# CONTENTS

{ ix }

{ x }

# THE PSYCHOLOGY OF
# EVERYDAY LIVING

# PART I

## SUCCESSFUL LIVING—OUR ATTITUDES AND EMOTIONS

There is no sure-fire formula for successful living. There are definite techniques, however, which can help us to live successfully. Although financial achievement is important, it is not the only factor. Our happiness depends on our ability to solve numerous problems of adjustment to the world. Each day may bring new and unexpected challenges.

Unfortunately, our system of education does not provide adequate training in the fine art of successful living. That training would emphasize subjects such as: how to live with yourself; how to plan your life; how to make decisions; how to become tolerant and learn to get along with others; how to face responsibilities. Consideration of the psychological principles related to these subjects should help us to meet successfully the major tasks and problems of everyday living.

To discover these psychological principles, we interviewed more than ten thousand "average" citizens. One of the first things we learned is that most of them had some kind of personal ideal—some perfect model—which they tried to imitate. Their ideal invariably had a profound influence on their attitudes, points of view, and accomplishments.

11

*Western Ways Photo*

Human beings have retained forms of behavior which lost their functional significance thousands of years ago.

# Are you your own ideal?

We all compare ourselves occasionally with our ideal. We look into the mirror to compare our profiles with the perfect lines we would like to see. At times we wonder how intelligent, charming, sociable, and efficient we really are, and we feel disappointed at the results of our self-evaluation.

Mr. Brown, one of our respondents, reported an experience which illustrates what happens when people cannot match their ideal. He was quite an eloquent and convincing speaker when in a small group. Then, one day, he was called on to address a meeting of several hundred people. After the first few sentences of his speech, he grew flustered and realized that he did not know how to continue. His attempt was a fiasco, and for a long time thereafter he was unable to speak effectively to even the smallest group.

Sometimes, however, people live up to, or even exceed, their ideal expectations. An elderly lady who had never before handled tools was forced to accept a job in an industrial plant. To her great surprise she discovered that she had considerable mechanical skill. This discovery gave her self-confidence, and she decided to make a career of technical work. In this career she became highly successful.

How can we explain our erroneous evaluations of our-selves? Why can we not see ourselves as we really are? Per-haps the primary cause is our feeling of the need for self-protection. Often we fear to discover all our shortcomings. In our constant efforts to adjust ourselves to the problems of everyday living, our main assets consist of our own abilities and attitudes—our personalities. Some of us feel much more secure if we never bother to look at our "psychological es-tate." We can then build the illusion that it is tremendous, inexhaustible. Others among us are afraid to use all our powers, and we live as if we had no ability. Both attitudes are based on feelings of insecurity, of fear that our real self is not to be trusted.

People who are emotionally well-balanced adapt their goals in life to their real capacities. They set up reasonable ambitions which are not too far beyond their reach. Over-ambitious people, as well as those who lack ambition, tend to follow very distant ideals and goals. They cannot relax. They strive for things beyond their grasp. Their goals are too difficult to attain. They are perfectionists, who see and magnify all their insufficiencies—minor and major. Com-pared with their ideal, they seem almost unbearably in-adequate.

## Can You Live with Yourself?

Some people have a negative picture of themselves. They see themselves as inefficient and disliked individuals. Often they do everything in their power to demonstrate to them-selves and to others that they are unworthy. Like the man who ignores his faults, these self-deprecating persons try to cover up reality. Even the man who humiliates himself does so because he thus derives psychological relief. He buys his way out of any responsibility to change himself.

{ 4 }

"I myself admit that I am no good," he says, "but I can't change, so leave me alone."

## Can You Learn to Like Yourself?

Among the mentally ill, there are those who feel completely at peace with themselves and the world. A patient who is thoroughly convinced that he is Napoleon admires himself and feels perfectly satisfied. He has achieved a perfect merger between his ideal and his personality. Most of us, fortunately, never reach this stage of complete unity between ideal and reality. The distance between our ideal and what we think we are should be constantly changing. If we become too ambitious, however, our successes fall far short of our dreams, and we feel that we have failed; the sense of failure handicaps us in our further efforts. We should, therefore, appraise our abilities and shortcomings realistically, and strive to achieve only reasonable ideals.

## Suggestions

Set up a reasonable ideal for yourself, one that you can expect to reach by using your capacities to the fullest extent. The best way to reach remote goals is to take care of immediate opportunities. The future will then take care of itself. Be ever ready to admit your own shortcomings. Attempts to ignore or to conceal them will handicap you in your progress toward a reasonable ideal. Nor should you fail to appreciate your full potentialities. When you reach one step on your ladder of achievement, you will be ready for the next higher rung. Avoid the temptation to become a perfectionist. In everyday living follow the rule of moderation. Strive to be practical and realistic, dealing not with conditions as they might exist in the distant future but as they exist today. The center of our universe is here and now.

# ARE YOU RUNNING AWAY?

There are many ways to run away from reality. We can try to escape or to postpone meeting the difficult circumstances or problems of life. Like other animals, when we are confronted with danger, we can stand our ground and attack, or we can run away. The psychologist's term for running away from reality is *escapism*. Psychological experiments have proved that all human beings react to danger in the two ways just mentioned. Thus, subjects in the experiments were unexpectedly shocked by an electric current. One group tightened their lips, tensed all their muscles, and looked as though they were ready to defend themselves. The other group reacted in just the opposite fashion. They loosened and dropped their lips, became limp and weak, and looked as though they were ready to surrender.

The great scientist Charles Darwin pointed out that human beings have retained certain forms of behavior which were once useful, but which lost their functional significance thousands of years ago. When angry, we may gnash our teeth or clench our fists. We do not usually bite our enemies —though sometimes an enraged person will do so—but we still use gestures which are relics of primitive behavior. Escapism is not, however, an attempt to avoid problems altogether. It is rather an effort to solve problems in a most inadequate and devious way. An animal running away from danger considers his action the safest way to solve the problem. Actually, running away is merely a manifestation of psychological uncertainty. This is sensed clearly by the aggressor, who promptly sets out in pursuit of his victim as soon as the latter shows signs of fear. The victim's fear is intensified as he seeks to escape.

We moderns are not very far removed from primitive man. We no longer seek to escape our problems by running away in a physical sense. Often we conceal the fact that we are even trying to evade responsibilities. So we concoct plausible excuses for our failure to cope directly with difficulties. The "sour grapes" attitude is one of the most common forms of such rationalization. One of our respondents sought advice as to the advisability of changing his occupation. "I seem to have got into a rut," he said. "I wonder whether the trade I am in has something to do with it. I am a pressman in a printing shop. Somehow I have the feeling that this line doesn't offer enough interesting work for me. I would like to get out of it and learn something new." This sounded convincing, but further inquiry revealed the "sour grapes" attitude. His present job required exceptional effort for advancement, and he had convinced himself that the effort was not worth while.

There are numerous kinds of escapism. Thus, people say they cannot get ahead because they lack will power or intelligence. Such confessions may seem rather justifiable, at first glance, but analysis usually shows them to be merely clever attempts to camouflage escapist tendencies. How easy it is for people to admit that they are lazy, for this relieves them of responsibilities. They can sit back and ignore difficulties.

*Ewing Galloway*

City people dream about recreation in the country, while rural people talk about an "easy job in the city." But country life is not all recreation, and work in the city has its problems and disadvantages.

## Suggestions

Distinguish between reasonable ambitions and merely fanciful dreams. City people who dream about the advantages of living on a farm should realize that farming is no sinecure these days, but actually a difficult and challenging career. Rural people who talk about an "easy job in the city, where you can quit at 5 P.M., enjoy your week-ends, and receive your salary check without having to worry about feed prices and poultry diseases," should wake up to the complex problems and disadvantages of urban life.

Do not rely too much on the moving pictures, "soap operas," or drink to help you solve real problems. Instead of seeking remote goals and overambitious ideals, which are often stimulated by moving-picture phantasies or by drink, concentrate on deciding what your immediate problems are, and start doing something about them. It is quite all right to see an inspiring moving picture or drama once in a while, but you should analyze these experiences to discover which of the incidents, if any, might apply to your personality and problems. If none of them applies, don't waste time dreaming about them.

Put yourself on an "emotional diet." If you feel the need of escape and relaxation, set time limits for these experiences. Well-planned relaxation of this kind will help you to gain renewed vigor to face your problems of life, after the brief period of emotional therapy, and to avoid loafing, daydreaming, and other forms of escapism.

One of the best ways to get rid of escapist tendencies is to adopt a realistic attitude toward your accomplishments. Keep a record of what you have achieved and strive to better that record. Do not compare yourself with other people. Instead, compare yourself of yesterday with yourself of today.

ARE YOU A FATALIST?

Few indeed are the people who have not been tempted, at one time or another, to adopt a fatalistic attitude. Such an attitude is rewarding, in the sense that it makes us think that a good many of our troubles have been solved for us. We can sympathize with the person who, when faced with difficult tasks requiring utmost intelligence and effort, says: "It is all written in the stars, anyway. My own efforts will not make much difference." The moment he has said this and has accepted it as true, he can relax and his disturbed mind can rest in peace.

Perhaps this narcotic effect of fatalistic submission explains why, again and again in world history, there have been developed religions and philosophical systems which encourage fatalism. Poets have written much about the futility of human affairs. Omar Khayyam wrote:

> *With Earth's first Clay They did the Last Man knead,*
> *And there of the Last Harvest sow'd the Seed;*
> *And the first Morning of Creation wrote*
> *What the Last Dawn of reckoning shall read.*

The question may be asked, Is fatalism inevitable? The answer is that fatalism is psychologically avoidable. Furthermore, despite the widespread desire of human beings for complete submission to the will of a Superior Force, a Fate, or God, our whole personality rebels against perfect passivity. Men are torn psychologically between reliance, upon the one hand, on a superhuman force determining human destiny and reliance, on the other hand, upon their own power to mold that destiny for themselves. In their refusal to accept fatalism completely, they have sought to unlock the innermost secrets of Nature, as witness recent successful efforts to find the atomic key to the universe. What does the progress of science represent, if not man's attempt to become the effective ruler of his world and master of his fate? This attempt is nothing new, for even primitive tribesmen, realizing their own impotence, sought to influence their God of Rain and Sun to provide for the needs and wishes of humble suppliants on earth.

The average person wishes to be master of his own destiny. He is eager to learn all the "tricks of the trade" of living. At the same time, he often seizes upon fatalistic excuses for lack of accomplishment. And yet, he will not openly admit his fatalistic attitude. Furthermore, he realizes that self-help is necessary for successful living. Rarely, nowadays, do we find anyone who depends completely on his Kismet or his star.

Many people, however, translate old-fashioned fatalism into modern terms. "I don't seem to have the right approach to people," said one of our young respondents. "I always get nervous and all flustered, and have a hard time speaking to strangers. And often I wish so hard I could be relaxed, especially when I meet a nice girl. I am quite aware of the poor impression I am making on her. But what can I do about it? It must be something in me that is causing all this. I guess it is my feeling of inferiority." Actually, this young man had been demoted in his job, and this had caused him to develop an inferiority complex. But how reasonable his statement sounds—until we begin to analyze it! All such explanations are merely *apology gremlins*. If we lack courage to face our problems, we tend to formulate these high-sounding apologies, instead of vigorously attacking our problems. People who realize the absurdity of setting up plausible excuses for failure—excuses which merely impede successful living—will begin to appraise their problems realistically and get busy doing something about them.

A fatalistic attitude is particularly dangerous in the area of broad social and world problems. Many of us throw up our hands and do nothing about problems of mass poverty, ill health, and war. Thus, often we hear the remarks: "What can I do to prevent war? The forces that cause war are irresistible. The individual is helpless. That demon, war, is inevitable." Actually, the demon is caused by the inaction of well-meaning individuals everywhere who, instead of trying to meet this crucial problem, pass it over to their apology gremlins.

*Suggestions*

Some degree of fatalism may be unavoidable. But an attitude of extreme submission to fate is both undesirable and easily avoidable. Such an attitude represents an effort to avoid one's responsibilities by posing as a helpless victim of some uncontrollable power. You can solve your problems if you face reality and depend on yourself. Self-reliance is the only way to achieve security and progress.

# HOW TO MAKE DECISIONS

Young Miss White came to a psychologist for advice as to which of three men she should marry. It was a difficult decision for her to make. "I like every one of them," she said. When the psychologist suggested Joe, she replied that she would miss Bill and Peter too much. She made similar remarks about the alternative choices. In brief, she just could not make up her mind. How frequently most of us feel the same way when confronted with dilemmas that require prompt decisions! Such a challenge affects different people differently, but few enjoy the situation. Why does the inability to make an immediate decision disturb us emotionally?

The answer is to be found, not in the choices we must make, but within ourselves. The psychologist consulted by our puzzled Miss White realized that she would not be helped to arrive at a decision by the suggestion that she make further comparisons among her three suitors. He explained to her that she was really afraid to make *any* choice—that she feared the finality of a decision. She had three suitors, with all her dreams and hopes attached to them. Once she had decided in favor of one, she would have only him, but refusing to decide, she still left open all three possibilities. Thus, in a thwarted fashion, she derived a feeling of security from her indecision.

Suppose we have to decide between our present job and a new one. What do we do psychologically? We paint a mental picture of all the advantages the new job may offer: more pay, greater authority, and a nicer office. But perhaps our present job offers more security, in that we are thoroughly familiar with its requirements and with our associates. Perhaps easier working conditions compensate somewhat for the difference in salary offered. In making a decision, we go through a sort of quick accounting procedure, listing the main advantages and disadvantages of each possible course of action. Too often, however, we overlook certain factors which are not readily apparent—psychological influences partly submerged in our minds. Thus, in deciding between two jobs, some of us may be swayed by our fear of change or by our lack of courage to start anew.

As soon as we discover the true causes of our indecision, we can sincerely weigh and consider the arguments for and against each alternative. The man who learns that his own fear of change is the major obstacle to further progress can do something to counteract his fear. Frequently, so far as successful living is concerned, this kind of self-analysis and self-redirection is more useful than the concrete advantages of a new job. Naturally, there are times when a decision is extremely hard to make. Sometimes the merits of one choice may be about equal to those of another. Further, there may be a gap between the imagined and the real advantages of each alternative, as when some people in the city dream about the wonderful life of farmers while rural people long for the comforts of the city.

"Acting out" the various alternatives is generally helpful. For example, new proposals may be tried out on a small

{ 14 }

Lecturers try out their speeches at home.

scale, as when people rent a house for a few months before buying it. Lecturers try out their speeches at home before facing their audiences. Salesmen act out what they will say if their prospective customers ask questions about their products. Young people try to forecast what may happen if they marry, and often they act out many phases of life together before tying the knot. If, despite everything we can do, we still find it hard to make a decision, we should choose arbitrarily and then make the best of it. Then, if we ignore the possible advantages that we had uncovered in the alternative choices, we shall feel happier through having gotten rid of uncertainty and doubt. We shall form the habit of facing life problems realistically and accepting the consequences.

*Suggestions*

In attempting to make decisions, do not be misled by superficial pros and cons. Analyze yourself, to discover the underlying causes of your indecision. So far as possible, act out all the alternatives. You may discover new factors that will influence your decision. Examine all the possible disadvantages of any choice that you consider making. Reject the temptation to rationalize in order to explain or justify your decision. Do your best, make a decision, and then make the best of it.

Avoid fear of the unknown, of change and experiment. It is one thing to embark upon a reckless course of action merely because you are bored with the *status quo*. Fools rush in where wise men fear to tread. But it is quite another and proper thing to try out practical decisions based upon facts and careful thinking. Remember that lasting progress depends upon your efforts to introduce wise changes and to improve upon imperfect habits and unsatisfactory conditions. Do not hesitate to act on the basis of careful decisions.

# Create your own TOMORROW

Have you ever stopped to wonder why children get excited about many things which leave adults cold? Whatever they do, wherever they go, children always anticipate a thrilling experience. They expect miracles. Every minute is to them a promise of a better tomorrow, and life is full of pleasant surprises.

We adults grow old too soon. We become cynical and bored. Nothing can surprise us any more—except unpleasantly. We are afraid of tomorrow, for it is the unknown, the uncharted, which threatens events beyond our control. In Europe, during the long years of the recent war, some people were afraid to turn on the radio. They had heard so much bad news that they had come to regard radio as a device for tuning in on their hopeless fate. Had they surrendered entirely to such feelings of futility, they would have despaired. Instead, while the Nazi boasted he would rule a thousand years, these people quietly prepared for tomorrow. At first, preparation meant just to succeed in hiding and surviving, but, later on, counterattack became possible. These freedom-loving men had understood how to get ready to build their tomorrow.

Even in everyday, non-heroic ways, it is desirable and helpful to build our own tomorrow. Why not look forward to interesting things we can do in the immediate future? If there is nothing particularly appealing in our plans, this means we are missing something important. We have neglected an essential rule: Successful living requires variety and surprises. How fast time flies when we have some fine achievement to look forward to!

For instance, according to research on the best methods of studying, we should vary the subjects we study, so that we will always be able to choose from among a number of subjects. In this way, we can look forward to new, interesting tasks. While we work at one task, we build the next surprise for ourselves. Many people, however, force themselves to repeat the same activities day after day. Psychological experiments show that there is no need for such rigid discipline. As a matter of fact, permitting a worker to create his own expectations, and to experience new stimuli, leads to greater efficiency. Even in prosaic tasks, like housecleaning, the modern homemaker can introduce numerous variations and surprises. She can try out new products that are constantly being put on the market. She can vary the order of her work. She can rearrange furniture. She can even skip the cleaning entirely every once in a while. These simple devices will give her the pleasure of variety, of meeting the unexpected.

## Suggestions

Life moves ahead. Those of us who look backward instead of forward are acting contrary to Nature, for we are negating life. We should not wait for whatever tomorrow may bring forth, but should rather plant the seeds of our own surprises. Life will then cease to be a fated experience over which we have no control; it will consist of a series of definite steps leading us to new fields of interest and surprising tomorrows.

# HOW DO YOU MEET CHALLENGES ?

Mr. Brown had just been promoted. He had been waiting months for this event. All his efforts had been pointed in this direction. Finally, his dream had come true. He should have been overjoyed, for he had been successful. Instead, his feelings were not at all those of a happy person. He became jittery, nervous, depressed. He was unable to explain it. What had happened? How account for his state of mind? Was he afraid of success?

Consider another case. A young man reported that his boss had decided to send him away for a three weeks' vacation because he showed signs of a nervous breakdown. This neurosis developed shortly after he had been promoted to the position of manager of his department. At first, the young man could see no connection between his symptoms and his promotion. He felt that it was just an unfortunate coincidence that his ailment had come at a most inopportune time. Actually, his symptoms served a most useful purpose in his own mind: they relieved him of having to face the risk of failure in a new and more responsible position. He could now hide behind his symptoms so that no one would discover that he was not ready to assume new responsibilities.

In meeting any kind of serious problem, we are all subject to this same fear of failure. It is a common fear among young people about to get married. How often a sudden panic grips bride, or groom, or both! Each begins to doubt that it will be possible to live up to the other's expectations.

A salesman in a progressive business organization complained about having gotten into a rut. Everyone but him had been promoted to a better job. A study of his remarks revealed that he himself was responsible for his situation. Whenever anyone praised his work, or mentioned the idea of promoting him, his sales record became poor. Without being aware of it, he slowed down and blocked his own progress, in order to stay on in his relatively comfortable position. He felt vaguely afraid that he would be unable to do what would be expected of him if he were promoted. Fortunately, a new department manager arrived who was enough of a psychologist to guess the fears which had kept this salesman from getting ahead. The manager discussed the situation with the salesman, and explained the facts to him. Then the manager promoted him to the position of district supervisor. Knowing that the new manager had confidence in him, the salesman soon developed self-assurance and demonstrated excellent ability.

*Suggestions*

Without fear, accept the challenge of possible failure. If necessary, learn to accept defeat sometimes. Strangely enough, acceptance and acknowledgment of personal shortcomings will help you to achieve success. In other words, be satisfied with reasonable accomplishment; don't be a perfectionist. Set your aim within your reach—then attain it.

As you accept new challenges, stop worrying about losing what you now have. Do more of the things you want to do.

Look upward to further achievements on the ladder of life. Never look downward to see how high you have climbed. Keep moving in an upward direction.

The salesman developed self-assurance and ability.

What is your GOAL in life?

"When I grow up, I'll be a plumber," said a four-year-old boy. When we asked him why, he replied, "Then I can make the water run wherever I want to. And people will have to call me when it is cold in the house, too." Even in such childish remarks we can find basic psychological factors which influence our goals in life. No matter what our desires appear to be on the surface, all of them represent some form of adaptation to our environment and to the exigencies of life. The answer to the question, What do we want most out of life? is that we want to adjust ourselves to life in such a way that our survival shall be for the longest possible period of time.

This simple concept of survival has been masked and embellished in many ways by our modern civilization. A boy who wants to become an engineer knows that this occupation will provide him with a means for controlling the forces which surround him, and eventually for mastering other human beings who are part of the environment to which he must adjust himself. Instinctively, he feels that his abilities as an engineer will give him a feeling of security and power and thus insure his survival.

We are no longer content, however, with purely physical survival. We want more than that. We want to preserve our individual tastes, and ways of living—our personalities. We want not only to satisfy our hunger, but also to satisfy our emotional desires and our refined appetites. If we ask people what they want most out of life, they answer with vague generalities, such as security or happiness. Goals such as wealth, fame, and good health would be more to the point.

In many cases, we can determine what a man really wants by observing what he *does,* rather than by listening to what he *says.* Some time ago, a young man who had difficulty finishing college came to a psychologist for advice. He could not force himself to study hard enough to pass his examinations. Yet, he claimed that his most ardent desire was to acquire a Ph.D. degree in English. By profession, he was a mediocre actor and he realized that, if he could improve his education, he might be able to become a theatrical producer. He was so eager about his goal in life that there was not much doubt about the sincerity of his plans. But why couldn't he make good? During the interview, he refused to talk about his study habits. Finally, the psychologist decided to prepare the young man's assignments with him. The psychologist noted that the youth had formed the peculiar habit of stacking about fifteen books on the desk, just before sitting down to study, and in addition, all his copybooks and notes. Then the young fellow would begin to think about which book he should open first, and where he should start. To make this decision, he opened each book and inspected all his copybooks. Before he could settle down to work, the time he had set aside for study had elapsed. When the period ended, he realized the tremendous task still ahead. As a result, he had a feeling of deep disappointment and utter failure.

At first glance, it would seem that this young man simply did not know how to organize his studies. But there was more to it than that. He did not really want to succeed in his studies; despite all his declarations to the contrary, he did not want to pass the examinations. Everything he did made it impossible for him to reach the highly desired Ph.D. degree. He knew that he had not been very successful as an actor. True, the possession of a literary degree might prove that his failure as an actor was attributable mainly to his having chosen the wrong occupation. But if he should get his degree, and still not be successful in a new occupation, he would have to admit, even to himself, that his failure was fundamental and inescapable. Rather than expose himself to this terrifying possibility, he sabotaged his avowed goal and worked secretly toward his partly submerged goal of *not* succeeding. This case illustrates the relationship between a professed goal and a real one.

If a young lady says she yearns for the slim figure of a moving-picture star, her interest in that goal seems to be sincere and believable. Before accepting her statement that this is her real goal, however, we should ask what she is doing about it. If she reports that ever so often she fails to follow her reducing diet, or that she can never resist a piece of cake offered to her, we are entitled to conclude that she does not really want to reduce. In other words, we really desire a goal only if we are willing to take the detailed, and sometimes very exacting, steps necessary for achieving it. In everyday living casual interest must be definitely distinguished from major purposes.

There is a continuous line from our desire and dreams to an actual goal. Each part of this line is linked with the next by many little steps which we may call "immediate goals." They are necessary if we are to reach the "remote goal."

What is her real goal in life?

Many people, if they fully realized that their ambitions have to be translated into these immediate day-by-day achievements, would readjust their ambitions. We wonder how many men are plaguing themselves with aspirations which they think of as true goals, while, in actuality, they loathe them. They cannot see this clearly, because they have only the shining result in mind. This bright dream, when reached, very often turns out to be quite disappointing. In a sense, it never existed in just the way in which these people thought of it.

For example, if an individual's goal is wealth, he will translate this dream into planning years of struggle, hard work, constant aggression, and defense of whatever he has acquired. If good health is his goal, he must think of sacrificing certain pleasures, disciplining himself as to habits of living; often he will find such immediate goals unpleasant. One of the major problems of everyday living is that of developing the ability to forego immediate gratifications and to endure temporary unpleasantness, in order to reach desired goals. Life consists of setting up goals, then either reaching them or giving them up, and, finally, setting up new goals.

Some people work diligently and courageously to achieve the goal they have set for themselves. Others go only halfway in attacking the problem. Then they try devious methods for getting around the apparently unattainable goal; they look for easier approaches. Still others assume a "sour grapes" attitude, or the equivalent of it. Instead of achieving their real aims, they establish a pseudo-goal for themselves, one which may look like the original high-sounding aspiration but is actually far from it.

The direct approach to the problems of life is the easiest and shortest road. As we approach a goal, often it becomes less forbidding and less difficult than we had imagined. Unfortunately, many of us suffer from a wrong perspective. A task of any magnitude should be seen under a "diminishing" glass. Looking at it from our usual point of view, with all the distance between our resolution and the final aim, we see the problems magnified. We should take this fact into account and concentrate on the difficulty of each immediate step on the road to our goal. We should not be overwhelmed by the apparent enormity of the total task.

## Suggestions

When you have set your heart on any kind of ambition, be it a Hollywood figure, wealth, or good health, be sure to translate this dream into its real meaning. Consider what action you need to take today, in order to approach your remote goal. What are the immediate goals you should work toward? Then, when you think of the sacrifices your goal will require every day, consider the advisability of changing your objective.

It is a sign of maturity to be able to look beyond momentary satisfactions. The cake you don't eat today may supply you with years of future happiness. So decide what you want most out of life. Do you really want just momentary satisfactions? Or do you prefer the more lasting satisfactions of an intelligently planned life, rich in achievement? If the latter, are you willing to make the necessary sacrifice and effort?

"Why, you are such nice people! I'd never have thought that you are Jewish," the Negro maid said to her employer. The maid seemed quite unaware of the insult implied in her remark. "Have you ever had bad experience with Jewish people?" the employer asked her. "Oh, no," came the reply. "I would never have worked for Jewish people if I had known it in advance, so I really couldn't say that they have harmed me. But everybody knows that they don't treat you in a fair way."

Such remarks can be heard often, and not always are they made by Negroes about Jews. Sometimes, the same things are said by Jews about colored people, by Catholics about Protestants or vice versa, and by native Americans about foreigners. The list is an endless one, and the psychological formula behind all such accusations is the same. The main cause of intolerance is fear of the strange, unknown, or different kind of person representing another race or nationality.

Experiments in child psychology have shown that, up to a certain age, a child is frightened when he sees an adult friend put on a mask. The child cannot recognize the familiar voice coming from behind the weird face. When the mask

{ 28 ∫

is taken off, he forgets his fears and responds again to his familiar, smiling friend. We all tend to be afraid of persons or situations unknown to us. This is a protective measure. A certain caution in dealing with new situations and problems helps to prevent our making serious mistakes.

Psychological studies analyzing the food preferences of people show that the higher an individual's intelligence and the broader his experience, the more readily will he try new kinds of foods. A primitive tribesman is afraid to eat food that is new to him. A sophisticated world traveler, however, will savor the delicacies of strange countries and will seek variety, instead of his customary menus. He has learned to recognize familiar taste pleasures within each national recipe. His freedom from fear leads to increased pleasures.

Individuals who feel insecure tend to regard as a menace all people with a different skin color or unfamiliar manners. But intolerance is not restricted to racial and national differences. No two human beings are exactly alike. Each has his peculiarities and individual mannerisms. Intolerant people reject the right of others to be different. They may be annoyed by even trifling differences. Thus, if these critics are more efficient in the mornings, they resent people who work best at night. If they like to wear a hat, they consider a hatless person a queer or dangerous character.

Intolerance may also be directed against oneself. A certain young man worried about his habit of feeling downhearted every once in a while, even though he knew from experience that he would recover from his despondency within a day or two. Still, he felt uncomfortable, for he believed that his changing moods made him different from others. In this sense, he was intolerant toward himself. Many people are intolerant of their own shortcomings. They feel dissatisfied because of insecurity and lack of self-confidence.

*How Can We Develop Tolerance?*

Beasts of the jungle, too, are intolerant. They do not allow strange animals to come near them. Their range of experience is narrow, so whatever looks unfamiliar to them is automatically considered a potential enemy. Domesticated animals, on the contrary, tend to display confidence. Instead of being frightened by unfamiliar creatures, they are interested in them, sniff them, and decide whether they are dealing with friend or foe. Young children react in much the same way. They watch one another critically at first, until they get acquainted. When adults meet strangers at a party, they do the same thing but in a sophisticated manner. They try to find out everybody's name, business, marital status, and social importance. If they succeed, then they feel that these people are no longer mysterious, perhaps awe-inspiring, strangers.

It seems, therefore, that a degree of intolerance is unavoidable. It is not easy to be tolerant. It is as hard to get rid of prejudice as it is to get rid of fear. This is a bad state of affairs, because fear increases intolerance, and vice versa. Fortunately, there are ways to break this vicious circle, and to reduce or eradicate a great many fears and prejudices simultaneously.

You can train yourself systematically in tolerance. Spend some time with members of nationalities other than your own. Read books about the customs and habits of other peoples—preferably books written by themselves; perhaps you can study a foreign language and read such literature in that language. Go to see moving pictures which were produced in foreign countries. Go to museums and study both ancient and modern cultures.

Strangely enough, your efforts to understand others will enrich your understanding of your own national or cultural group. You will discover many similarities between your own group and others. Part of their culture will become your own. Understanding that all human beings belong to the same family will increase your feeling of security. You will feel as if your own power and effectiveness had been increased manyfold through association with the power and talent of many other peoples. Remember that intolerance deprives you of human resources which should be the shared possessions of all mankind. Tolerance brings its own rewards in many personal ways. It makes us stronger spiritually. It leads to a wider recognition and acceptance of our own limitations and those of our intimate associates. Bear in mind that there is a kernel of justification or significance in what you consider even the most absurd attitudes in others. Your increased understanding of human nature will help you to meet successfully the problems of everyday living.

## Suggestions

When you meet strangers, concentrate on efforts to discover their basic human values. Disregard superficial characteristics, such as income or nationality. Investigate the "psychological race" of the individual. There are people with attitudes which have nothing to do with membership in a particular race or creed—some with a spirit of humanity and kind understanding, others with a spirit of arrogance or hatred. The latter feel superior, and set themselves apart from the rest of the community. They belong to a different "psychological race." You should learn to distinguish between real *racial* types in this sense of the term. These factors of character matter much more in the realities of life than superficial variations in skin color or family origin. Follow the example of scientists who, when they attend international conventions, forget national differences, even though so many different languages may be spoken that the services of interpreters are essential to a mutual understanding.

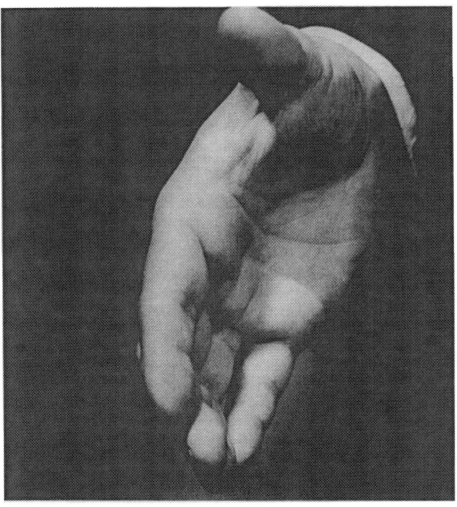

Extending the hand of fellowship.

## Do you really LIVE TOGETHER ?

It was Tommy's and Susan's fifth wedding anniversary. They had been out celebrating, and had had fun. When they came home, late at night, both were tired and in a meditative mood. Finally, Susan asked questions which had been in both their minds: "Do you think ours has been a good marriage? Will our children say, in future years, that they had a good family life?" Tommy and Susan had quarreled now and then. At times they had felt bored with each other. Tommy might have been impatient, or Susan might have been nervous and irritable. Tommy could make up a long list of things which he wished they had done differently, and so could Susan. Yes, he had looked at other girls. He had always liked beautiful legs. She could be accused of having dreamt once in a while of a rich fellow who might have married her.

What makes family life wholesome and successful? Experts disagree. Some say complete freedom of partners; others say this would be the worst possible thing. Any expert will say that husbands should be more attentive, praise their wives, and that wives should show interest in their husbands' work. The psychologist knows that these things all help; and certainly nothing can be said against the sharing of household duties, as in washing dishes or taking care of the children.

But these suggestions touch only the surface of the problem. At times, they may even imply recourse to forms of bribery and artificiality. To understand the factors making for successful marriage, we must consider basic psychological influences. We should try to find out why people get married, and what they expect to get out of marriage. Love and romance—in a sense, yes. But let us forget, for a moment, the romantic ideas built up in our minds by moving pictures and fiction. To the scientist, marriage is a biological process. People marry to bring up children, who will perpetuate the race. But what does marriage mean to the psychologist?

*Marriage Provides Security*

Two people who live and work well together achieve a more successful adaptation to the problems of life. Marriage is a form of social insurance. All human beings depend on affection, love, more than on anything else to help them muster courage and face life with all its perils of illness and misfortune. A frightened infant is eager to be kissed and hugged. He needs security. The same is true of adults. Romantic lovers may not realize that they are really seeking strength through love. As a part of life experience, marriage is governed by the dynamic principle that life is an ongoing, developing, growing process. From the moment of birth onward, we need protection and love. We get them from our mothers, then from other people in our family circle, and from our friends. Friendship represents an admixture of respect and affection. Eventually, we seek love and security by making a lifelong compact of marriage.

Mr. K—, who mistrusted his wife, came to consult a psychologist. He feared that she was not true to him, and he was extremely jealous. He had been unable to find out whether or not his fears were justified. The psychologist knew at once that, regardless of the facts of the case, Mr. K's marriage had not been a success. He had not derived from it the security and protection which he had expected. Nor was his wife responsible for the failure of their marriage. The fundamental cause originated in his childhood experiences. As a child, Mr. K— had been denied sincere affection. Later on, he was unable to trust the woman who did love him. Unfortunate experiences had warped his attitudes and made him unable to respond spontaneously to that affection without which no marriage can succeed.

One important criterion of the success of any marriage is, then, the feeling of security derived by both partners. In a successful marriage, this feeling should increase as the years go by. But security does not mean mutual dependency. Each partner should possess adequate strength and self-assurance, but should be ready to supplement the other's powers as the need arises. The question that should have been asked by Tommy and Susan—mentioned earlier—is this: Do we feel more married now than we did five years ago? In a successful marriage, with its coöperative striving toward plans and ideals, the feeling of security deepens through shared experience.

There is another criterion of successful family life: Does each partner accept the situation as reasonably worth while, or is there disappointment? If people miss the romantic glamor they expect from marriage, perhaps this is because their dream marriage—their ideal—was not also realistic, was not true to life. We should understand that marriage is a part of life experience, and must therefore include both the romance and the prosaic disappointments of life. Often, disillusionment is caused by mistaken points of view and un-

In a successful marriage the feeling of security increases as
the years go by.

justifiable expectations. People who are happily married accept life on its own terms. They know that the good and the bad constitute an interesting over-all pattern. Especially in homes blessed with children, there is always something new to look forward to, new plans, prospects, and accomplishments. Romance, basically, is nothing but the thrill of expectancy. Every day brings something new. We can all recreate and perpetuate zest in living by building our own tomorrow.

A young woman complained about her husband. No matter what she tried to do, he would not show any interest in her. When he came home from work, he would sit down and read the newspaper in silence. It would seem that one could not blame her for growing impatient and unhappy. In reality, however, she was chiefly to blame, for she had failed to interest herself in her husband's progress, and had done nothing to encourage him to advance himself. They had lived beside each other, but not really together. More than that, they had ignored another principle of the successful marriage—mutual adaptability. When he tried hard to get an education, she attempted to divert his attention from his studies to her own vague remarks and projects. She seemed to resent his educational program, as though it made his interests more worth while to him than association with her. He took revenge, if we may call such a subconscious process revenge, by withdrawing all his attention from her.

Blaming the other partner is a common unrealistic reaction to disappointments in married life. Seldom are there situations in which only one side is at fault. Such accusations reflect childish immaturity. When a child bumps into a table, he is tempted to strike the table in anger; adults have learned to modify their behavior so as to avoid collision. Incompatibility in marriage often means that neither partner has really tried to adapt to the other, but that both have followed their own childish impulses. In a successful marriage, both partners mold each other, and this is why constructive criticism, as distinct from fault-finding, is essential and should be welcomed. Unqualified admiration may be flattering, but it does not assure a happy marriage.

## Suggestions

Ask yourself whether or not your marriage partner has changed since your marriage. Have you improved your own personality? Remember the three major principles of a successful marriage: The first is the principle of dynamic development, constant adjustment to new circumstances. The second is the principle of realism, which implies that you should place your marriage squarely in the stream of life and accept its rough, as well as its smooth, aspects. The third is the principle of adaptability, a process of reciprocal influence which develops new desirable traits of personality.

Bear in mind that success in your marriage depends on you, not on mysterious gremlins or unexpected smoothing out of difficulties. Provided that a basic mutual sympathy led you to choose your partner, what you do and how you do it will determine the future of your marriage.

Think about family life as a continuous process. Instead of saying, "We have been married for the past five years," put it this way, "We kept marrying each other during the past five years." This is the point of view essential to growth and truly successful living.

It is interesting to note that the United States has a very high rate of divorce. In Canada the rate is only one divorce to one hundred sixty-one marriages. The American rate is one divorce to every seven marriages. The causes of this high rate of divorce include legal and social as well as psychological factors. But an understanding of the psychology of human relations would go far to remedy the emotional instability, tensions, and unsolved problems of family life that nourish the roots of broken homes.

# Are you frustrated?

Perhaps this question should read, How frustrated are you? All of us are frustrated. Our first lessons in cleanliness deprive us of certain primitive desires—cause certain frustrations. Our whole education—the progress of civilization—involves many more. We should understand the psychological explanations of frustration, for our attitudes and behavior are often profoundly affected by such experiences.

## What Is Frustration?

Refuse to give an eager child some ice cream and you will have an example of frustration. He will protest vigorously. Frustration and aggression are closely interrelated. When we have been kept waiting for someone a long time, and he finally arrives, our first reaction is to snap angrily at him. An employee who has been reprimanded by his boss may let off steam against his family when he gets home.

At times, however, aggression resulting from frustration may be directed toward oneself. In other words, we feel angry at ourselves. Often, we are inclined to blame the nearest object or person for our anger, which, in reality, may have originated in privations suffered some time ago.

If we do not receive enough love or attention, we may try to punish those whom we blame for such frustration. We may even do this by punishing ourselves. Among certain tribes, a son may commit suicide to avenge himself on his father. In our society, a boy may become ill or injure himself to spite his parents. We could cite innumerable examples of such reactions.

*Suggestions*

The best way to meet the problems of everyday living is to analyze the roots of our own behavior. We must gain insight into our motivations. Such insight can often be attained through an attempt to understand the behavior of others. People who have been frustrated tend to develop aggressive attitudes. Their aggression represents an effort to combat frustration, and is therefore, at least in principle, a desirable countermeasure. Unfortunately, however, their aggression is not properly channelized, but is misdirected. They should be helped to focus it on a tangible, attainable goal. Thus, they will be enabled to take the first step toward removing the initial cause of frustration. In other words, we suggest that you practice self-analysis as an aid in dealing with your major problems. Then you should formulate a plan with a realistic goal that is fairly easy to reach.

If you feel irritable, don't accept your behavior as an inexplicable mystery, but search for the cause. What you think is the origin of your irritability may be merely the last drop that made your emotional cup overflow; the actual cause may lie in some long-forgotten incident. When you discover the basic causes of your frustration, you can generally do something about them.

At times, a bit of self-indulgence helps. "To let off steam" offers temporary relief. The Ashantis, for example, provide for special occasions when they are allowed to express anger. Before you begin to imitate this custom, however, just say to yourself, "Today I am going to be cross with everyone I meet." You will then see your anger in its true light; it will look ridiculous to you. Similarly, if certain people irritate you, find out why you dislike them. Perhaps they frustrate you because you do not give them what they want. Only when you give love will you receive it.

Refuse to give a child some ice cream and you will have an example of frustration.

# Why WORRY?

"There is nothing the matter with you," a physician frequently says when his patient complains of certain disturbances. "You just worry too much." But the patient is seldom given the proper prescription. He is rarely told how to go about decreasing his worries.

Any of us who have been the recipients of such an admonition by a physician or a friend will agree with its correctness. "Ah!" we will say to ourselves, "I just will not care any more. I'll do as the doctor says, and not worry." It isn't long, however, before we start thinking about what the next week will bring, or whether we should have been more courteous the last time we saw our friends. In other words, we are right back where we started—worrying ourselves sick over what has been, and what will be.

Worrying is often confused with attempts to find solutions to a problem. The man who worries, however, seldom does any real planning in order to alleviate his worrying. His energies are wasted in thinking about the future and the past, rather than being used for meeting problems of the present.

One way to combat worrying is to concentrate on what is happening now, while it is happening. There are many things each of us should have done differently, and there will be many wrong decisions we shall make in the future, but right now, today, we can do at least a score of things and do them right. We can try to enjoy what is happening this very minute, and attempt to make the most of the present. Thus we can build a reserve of experiences which will be useful for solving worrisome problems. All our energy will be focused on immediate tasks so that we let the future take care of itself.

Another remedy for worry is to accept responsibility for dealing with our own problems. People who worry a great deal are usually too passive about the things that worry them most. They spend so much time thinking about what the future may bring that they fail to mobilize their energies to meet immediate challenges. They also generally fail in their efforts to avert the very evils which they anticipate.

It is wrong for a woman to worry constantly about what might happen if her husband were to lose his job, or if he were to become ill. She could get rid of such worrying by a sort of "active fatalism." There are certain immediate and practical things which she could do to avoid some of the dangers which she fears. She could guard against illness by feeding her husband and all the family properly and taking common-sense hygienic precautions. She could try to prepare for the possibility that her husband might lose his job. For instance, she might be able to increase her savings. This would give him a feeling of security.

There are, of course, hundreds of dangers over which we have little or no control. As we walk along the street, for instance, we might be struck down by some falling object. We may as well be fatalistic about such things, for there is nothing much we can do about them. So, when a problem can be attacked, we should be aggressively active; we should do

She could guard against illness by feeding the family properly.

something about it. Toward the unexpected dangers beyond our control, we should adopt a realistic or a fatalistic attitude.

Often, worrying is caused by a feeling of guilt. If we fail to meet a responsibility, we tend to feel guilty, and we worry about what may happen as a result of our neglect. On the other hand, a person who does whatever he can to meet his responsibilities will not have much time to worry about the other things, beyond his control.

Psychological analyses of worry show that the most frequent cause is self-pity, which, strange as it may seem, is a form of conceit. Usually the chronic worrier wants to be the center of attention, wants everyone to make things easier for him, and thinks that no misfortune should ever befall him. According to his theory, he deserves only the best that

} 44 {

life has to offer. But as soon as he starts thinking about others instead of himself, and begins helping them to solve their problems, he stops feeling sorry for himself and learns how to cope with his own problems, instead of just worrying about them. So, in helping others, he helps himself.

*Suggestions*

Don't glorify worry. Many people mistakenly think that worrying about a problem is the same as trying to solve it. They forget that the man who worries too much seldom does any real planning to alleviate his worrying. His energies are wasted in *fretting,* not used in *doing.* Concentrate on the here and now—not the past or the future. Substitute action for worry. Don't worry when you can't do anything about the cause of your worry. When a problem cannot even be attacked, sit back and relax. Don't pity yourself. Think more about other people, and try to help them. You will no longer live in your own small, self-centered world, but will have found your place in your community—in society.

When dealing with serious problems or emergencies of life, adopt an optimistic attitude. A pessimist may succeed but he must first overcome the handicap of his own pessimism. "Where there's life there's hope." Remember the story of the elderly gentleman who said: "I am an old man. I am ninety years old. I have had many troubles during my lifetime, but my greatest troubles were the ones that never happened." Are your troubles the ones that never happen?

# REDUCE YOUR INHIBITIONS

A certain salesman reported that he could not endure the nervous strain of riding in an elevator above the eighth floor. He was asked what would happen if he were unable to get out of the elevator before it reached a higher floor. "I would get panicky," he replied, "and perspire all over. The experience would make my next ride unbearable." This inhibition naturally interfered with his work.

Most inhibitions are not so obvious as this one. Frequently, people are quite unaware of the fundamental causes of their psychological blockades. They merely realize vaguely that some inner conflict or psychological obstruction stands in their way and prevents spontaneity of behavior. A young lady who was in no sense a prude confessed that she could never overcome her tendency to resist being kissed by her fiancé. She liked him very much, but some mysterious power seemed to keep her from doing what she really wanted to do.

Inhibitions prevent us from making full use of our abilities. The effect on one's personality reminds us of an automobile being driven with the brakes applied. No matter how much gas we give the car, it will never operate efficiently under these conditions. Still, the proper remedy is to release the brakes, not to take them out of the car. Similarly, human beings need a reasonable number of inhibitions, which are part of the price they pay for civilization. Young children have no inhibition about getting dirty; often, they seem to enjoy both the process and the after-effects. Our society finds sexual inhibitions necessary, but a child shows only a natural curiosity about such matters.

How do we develop inhibitions? A little girl standing at the curb of a sidewalk was overheard debating with herself as to whether or not she should step off into the street. She whispered to herself, "I should not go out into the street because the cars will hurt me." Finally, she turned and continued to walk on the sidewalk. Evidently her training in safety had checked her impulse. This is one way in which desirable inhibitions develop. The repeated warnings of parents sometimes become part of our psychological equipment. An inhibition is a sort of permanently built-in censor. In one sense, each of us carries everywhere with him the personalities of his parents and of other respected people, who influence his behavior, even though they may not be physically present. In time, we forget the sources of our inhibitions. The little girl who restrains her impulse to rush into the street may have forgotten all about the people who first led her to form such habits, and yet she may never lose the inhibition.

All of us are influenced by inhibitions whose origins we may be unable to recall. In fact, frequently we do not even realize that we are subject to such restraining influences. Psychologists have discovered, for instance, that most men have a slight interest in the male physique. The average man, however, is seldom aware of that interest and is even then unwilling to admit it. Among Americans it is not the

This little girl needs to develop a built-in censor.

custom for men to kiss each other in greeting, and we feel embarrassed when observing such behavior. Our training and experience inhibit any tendency to show mutual affection in this way.

Sometimes, however, men free themselves almost entirely from their inhibitions. Thus, if we observe the behavior of two friendly drunkards, we shall see how they have no qualms about manners. They hug and kiss each other and exchange affectionate embraces, without the slightest feeling of embarrassment. A similar freedom from inhibitions is achieved in dreams. In our dreams we experience thoughts which we would never tolerate during our waking hours. Perfectly respectable people may dream that they are unfaithful or criminal characters. If our behavior differs markedly from that pictured in our dreams, this shows that we have many inhibitions which control our primitive or undesirable impulses. The stronger our real desires, the more powerful are the inhibitions required to control them.

To measure the extent to which a person is inhibited, psychologists read aloud certain clue words (such as mother, father, love) and ask him to associate each word with another related word of his own. If he hesitates a long time before responding to a word, this pause indicates that an important inhibition is preventing the free flow of his ideas. Ordinary conversation may also disclose the presence of inhibitions. When a speaker changes the subject abruptly, without apparent reason, or suddenly becomes silent, we may guess at the inner conflicts or doubts that inhibit the expression of his ideas.

## Suggestions

Find out how many and what kinds of inhibitions you have. Analyze your likes and dislikes, your everyday behavior, for clues. Learn to distinguish between rationalizations and the real causes of your reactions. Do not be afraid to discover your inhibited desires. Inhibitions known to you can be controlled more easily than subconscious ones. Choose intelligently between desires to fulfill, on the one hand, and desires to reject and consciously inhibit, on the other.

Shakespeare's "To thine own self be true" may be good poetry, but it is not always good psychology. On the contrary, it is often important to fool ourselves. This does not mean closing our eyes to real problems; it means adopting psychological devices which will help solve those problems.

A man recovering from a broken leg is glad to use a crutch until the limb is mended. Why should we deny ourselves the use of a mental crutch now and then? Every parent falls back on simple psychological "tricks" in rearing his children. Business executives practice "management psychology" to keep employees satisfied and efficient. We can use the same techniques just as profitably on ourselves.

### Trick Your Unconscious Mind

Deep down in our unconscious is a kind of "monitor" which controls and influences many of our conscious actions. It is here that we bury things we want to forget, such as keeping an appointment with someone we dislike. The unconscious also holds clues to the positive side of our natures—our preferences, hopes, secret ambitions. We can trick our unconscious minds into telling us hidden truths about ourselves.

This is not so hard as it seems. We know a young woman

who could not decide between two admirers. The uncertainty weighed so heavily on her mind that we worked out a psychological trick to help her make a decision.

As we suggested, she observed herself carefully in actions in which her unconscious mind might reveal her real preferences. We discovered that Carl, one of the suitors, liked her in light-colored dresses, while Bob, the other, preferred dark ones. Without telling her why, we asked her to note how often she wore each type of dress. In a three-weeks period she put on dark dresses almost twice as often as light-colored ones. Then she herself found the explanation: She *unconsciously* preferred to be with Bob.

There are many ways to trick our minds to reveal such secrets. We can watch ourselves when we are alone, when we have had a few drinks; compare what we tell people about ourselves with the facts as we know them. Observation will disclose our weak spots, what we are trying to hide, what we are likely to exaggerate. This knowledge, though gained by trickery, can be put to honest use in building a happier, better-adjusted life.

### Make a Deal with Yourself

Many otherwise capable people often lose courage halfway through a job and stop or turn back. If we are reluctant to complete a task, we can promise ourselves a reward for completing it and set a definite goal. We can say: "I shall paint the wall up to this corner, then walk around the block. Whatever I do after that will be a voluntary extra." This applies to writing or bookkeeping or any other kind of work. A scientific manager uses his knowledge of work-incentives.

In a study on cigarette smoking, we found that psychological reward rather than physical pleasure counts with most smokers. This is particularly true with pipe smokers. A mechanic said: "After a few hours of working I knock off and have a pipeful of my favorite tobacco. Then I am ready to go again. I look forward to that pause."

Every situation affords an opportunity of striking such a bargain with ourselves. In mechanical work our reward may consist of rest periods at certain intervals. In mental work it may be a brisk walk. In housework it may be reading a few pages of a novel. In any case, our "deal" is one in which we are sure to profit.

*Be Tolerant with Yourself*

Although it would be simpler for us to admit our imperfections, human nature persists in the illusion that we *can* be perfect. We promise ourselves certain accomplishments—yet how often we fall short, achieving little but a feeling of inadequacy.

There is a simple way to make the "illusion of perfection" work, and still avoid discouragement. Whenever we set a goal, we should give ourselves a thirty per cent discount on whatever our expectations may be. For example, we may add two or three days to our first estimate of the time it will take to complete a job. If we keep getting up late in the morning, we can set the clock ahead fifteen minutes.

Making a psychological analysis for a cosmetics company, we talked with hundreds of women who had been discouraged by overglamorous advertising. In attempting to be as beautiful as Lana Turner, they had only been disillusioned. The cosmetics company had set the goal too high. When their advertising sounded a more realistic note—how to improve ordinary looks, not how to attain an impossible ideal—the results were more satisfactory.

Similarly, studies show that perfection of enunciation is

not necessarily a great asset for radio announcers. An occasional slip of the tongue and minor errors seem to give the commercial announcement greater conviction.

*Suggestions*

Permit yourself a certain degree of failure *in advance*. Thus you will eliminate a psychological hurdle which trips many who demand the impossible of themselves.

The old belief that you should stick to a job until you finish it, or that you shouldn't do more than one thing at a time, has been disproved in numerous psychological studies. We now know that switching from one job to another keeps up our interest in the tasks. If you have difficulty holding to a certain goal, consider changing your objective.

This is particularly important when you do creative work, though almost every job involves some creative thinking. If you are a businessman, you are not wasting time when you take a walk during business hours. Watch people—familiarize yourself with what they like, what makes them potential customers. You will come back to your desk refreshed, and you may gain new ideas that might not otherwise have occurred to you.

Break loose from your daily routine. Enrich your experiences. If you are an office worker, indulge in manual labor occasionally. Try writing an article or a radio script. Doing these things will give you new points of view for use in your regular work.

It is not sufficient to say, "Know yourself." Manage yourself. Your innermost feelings have the erratic qualities of a child's fantasies. Be tolerant with this youngster who composes so much of your being. Don't just preach at and fight with him. Give him systematic guidance and encourage him to reach his real goals.

"Independence, that's what I want. No one is going to order me around any longer. From now on I am going to be my own boss and I am going to have my own business."

It is estimated that almost a million veterans of the recent war feel this way about their future. If we add to this group the millions of civilians who are dreaming about a business of their own—a little shop, a service station, or a small chicken farm—we realize that we are dealing with a major problem of national importance.

The economic aspect of making a decision between being our own boss or remaining an employee is not to be considered lightly. Is it possible to reverse the trend towards the growth of big business? Can pensions, social security, paid vacations, and all the other minor and major advantages of working for a large enterprise be matched by the small independent operator?

As crucial as such economic questions may be, there is another factor to be considered, namely self-evaluation. Are we fit to be our own bosses?

If we do not succeed in our proud enterprise of independence, we may lose one of our brightest dreams. We may dissipate one of our greatest assets: hope. The man who has to give up his business and accept a job again, often feels that he is a failure. But can we predict with accuracy our chances of success? Yes, there is a way to estimate our chances. It will not provide an insurance policy against failure, but it will give us some basis for judgment. All we have to do is to ask ourselves a few questions. If we answer them truthfully, we may discover whether or not we are fit to be our own bosses.

### Are You a Planner or a Fatalist?

When we are in the woods and someone is guiding us, we don't have to pay much attention to the paths we are taking. Nor do we have to worry about where we are going. When we are alone, the picture changes. There are many signposts which we then find to be necessary but which we formerly ignored. We would soon get lost if we did not have a map and information about roads and routes.

The same is true of being in business for ourselves. We have to plan ahead, perhaps several years ahead. We have to build a clientele. We have to order merchandise long in advance of our need.

Some people leave many of their decisions to fate. Fatalism is pleasant. One is excused if anything goes wrong, for it was destiny that willed it so. An employee can afford to be fatalistic better than his boss, and in a sense his boss represents destiny or responsibility.

If we in our daily activities leave many things to their own course, if we hate to plan ahead, we are inclined to be fatalistic. Lack of foresight is evidence that we belong to the escapist type. This is one point against us in rating our ability to be our own bosses. If, on the other hand, we are known to our friends as systematic people who know what they want and usually get it, we have earned a point in our favor. A planner likes to review all the factors which may conceivably affect his plans. He will say to himself: "Next year I'd like to accomplish this, and here is the way I am going to do it—step 1, then 2, then 3." If this kind of thinking is strange to us, we should not consider ourselves good planners.

## Can You See the Employer's Side?

Mr. Reynolds had just married. His father-in-law had a small business manufacturing metal furniture. Reynolds often criticized adversely the way the business was being run. He talked about how he would manage it if he were in charge. Suddenly, when his father-in-law was taken ill, the young man was given his chance to manage the business. This experience was a revelation to him. He then realized that he had never really considered in detail all the factors involved in that business. His criticisms had been superficial. Now he developed a healthy respect for his father-in-law's abilities and he decided to keep his own job as a salesclerk.

Can we put ourselves in the place of an executive whom we envy or criticize? Do we appreciate the employer's side? Are we interested in it? Such curiosity may be another good measure of our ability to be our own bosses.

## How Easily Do You Give Up?

We should ask ourselves these questions: What was the most recent goal you wanted very much to achieve? Did you succeed? What happened when you were confronted with difficulties? Did you try again and again or did you resign yourself to the inevitable? If we are usually persistent, we can add another point to our score. But if we seldom pursue a goal to the bitter end, our ability to be our own boss is doubtful. Business is a continuous struggle. Even before we have attained one goal, we have to set out after the next one. Most business enterprises depend on this ability to overcome temporary failures.

### Do You Need Frequent Pats on the Back?

Mr. Jones was very sensitive to opinions about his work. He would do everything in his power to attract attention and a pat on the back for his accomplishments. He dreamed about going into business for himself. We dissuaded him because his need of constant praise was so urgent that he would not have been able to face the strain of being on his own. No one thinks of praising the employer, who has to wait a long time before success manifests itself. He must rely on his own ability to succeed, for he has no boss to tell him how good he is.

Do you always need applause for your work?

*Ewing Galloway*

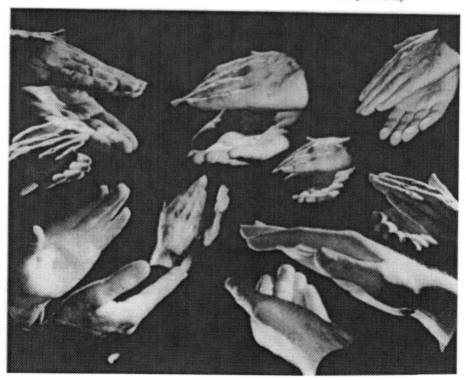

## Are You Imaginative?

No two businesses are exactly alike. Being one's own boss means that one has to adjust to all kinds of new situations. In competitive business the ability to contrive a new idea or method is half the battle. For instance, one imaginative go-getter, who noticed that housewives waste a great deal of time on individual shopping, became the village shopper—and a highly successful businessman. New ideas bring success. Other things being equal, those of us who possess a fertile imagination have a better chance to become successful bosses.

## Are You a Jack of All Trades?

An employee can afford to be a specialist. A boss has to be able to do many kinds of work. In some cases, he has to be an accountant, an advertising man, a salesman, a window display man, a typist, and an office manager, often a general handy man; last but not least, he has to be familiar with all the technical points about his field of business. If we have not done at least five different kinds of work, the chances are that we lack the versatility needed for running a modern business.

## Suggestions

Add up all your good points and all your bad ones. If you score on four or more of the criteria mentioned above, you have some assurance that you can succeed in your own business. Be sure to consider whether you want to be your own boss because you would really enjoy the challenge or are merely trying to escape the disadvantages of working for others.

Remember that a boss is in a sense just as dependent as an employee. Customers, competitors, wholesalers, and all the many other people with whom you will have to associate are often more demanding than the average employer.

There are many people, and you may be one of them, who complain about bad management. Employees tend to feel that they could put their talents to much better use in their own business. If you have a job in a firm which allows no one to use initiative and get ahead, start thinking about either changing your job or going into business for yourself. If you are unemployed, your decision should be based on two surveys: a study of conditions in your special field of interest, and an analysis of your own abilities and personality traits.

Both employers and employees need to learn how to get along with people. Both need to plan their work carefully, to be persistent, imaginative, and versatile. But the boss needs these qualities to an even greater degree than his employees, for his responsibilities are broader and more diversified.

Remember, too, that psychological assets alone do not insure success in business. In our competitive society, comparatively few business enterprises can grow without adequate resources, experienced management, and favorable economic conditions. Consider all these factors when you decide whether or not you should accept the great responsibility of going into business for yourself.

# How to feel good at the end of the day

How are you? Comment ça va? Cóme sta? In all languages all over the world, all day long people ask each other these questions. In doing so we talk about the mood of our friend. We are concerned or at least pretend to be interested in the feelings of happiness experienced by our companion. We seldom ask the other person: "Are you happy in your life or marriage?" unless we find ourselves on very intimate terms with him. We only want to know how he feels today. This fact has meaning. Our "HAPPINESS" spelled in capital letters is an abstraction. It is composed of many little things, such as the satisfaction derived from the coffee we had in the morning, or the first telephone call we received in the office, or how comfortable our shoes feel. The happiness of a whole year depends on the happiness of each month, each week, and each day. If we don't feel happy today and to-morrow and the day after that, how can we ever feel happy? This sounds like a platitude, and yet many people overlook this relationship between everyday satisfactions and the greatly desired goal of final happiness. "How to feel good at the end of the day," seems to be quite an important goal. How can it be done? What is the psychologist's answer?

## Voyage into the Unknown

The alarm clock has just stoically suffered our wrath and has wrapped itself in ominous silence. The shrill warning of the bell has been replaced by the silent but much more effective threat of the inescapable sweep of the second hand. We cannot escape it. We have to start on our 16-hour voyage into the unexplored future. Good things and bad things may happen to us. Everything is possible. Fear and hope mix within ourselves, as we look ahead into the day that awaits us.

We humans are cautious animals. We don't just let such a state of doubt repeat itself day after day. We take action. It is an unconscious, unplanned action, but it is there. We can notice it easily enough if we teach ourselves to observe sharply. Let's start with first things and see what people do at breakfast. We can't drop in on strange families at this hour of the day. But we can easily enough go down to the corner sandwich shop for an early snack or a bachelor's breakfast. And that is exactly what we did one morning recently.

The counterman took our order, but, as we waited for the bacon to crisp, we noted that he served other customers without waiting to hear what they wanted. A young woman at the end of the counter had coffee and toast set before her almost before she had settled on the stool. A portly gentleman who edged in next to us only grunted as he sat down, but the counterman quickly and correctly interpreted this as an order for two soft-boiled eggs. A young man murmured "the usual" and got it: cereal doused with cream.

These three regular customers and their counterman were acting out a little drama that is duplicated each morning at breakfast tables in thousands of American homes and at lunch counters and drugstores all across the country. To the practiced eye of the psychologist this ritual is significant.

Each of the three people at the counter was, without realizing it, taking the first step toward feeling good at the end of the day.

The counterman would be pretty sure what his "regulars" wanted to eat, because nine out of ten of us have substantially the same breakfast day in and day out. There is a simple psychological explanation for this. At breakfast we unconsciously establish a point of view for the entire day. Our regular automatic daily breakfast routine offers instinctive proof that although we're launched on a strange voyage, at least we're shipping out from a familiar port. The orange juice and coffee serve as symbolic signposts to tell us that everything is under control.

The fact that on a vacation or holiday or even Sundays we change our normal breakfast habits for a griddle cake and sausage splurge bolsters these conclusions. We enjoy a special treat at such times because we don't want that day to be like any other: We hope that something unusual will happen. But try breaking the morning routine on an ordinary blue Monday when the office opens at nine, and we may seriously disturb our emotional balance.

Even the foods we eat for breakfast are physical symbols of this psychological preparation for the journey. The steaming coffee helps us to warm up mentally as well as physically. Crunchy breakfast foods are more popular, advertising surveys show, than soft ones. Psychology explains this: People are reassured when they succeed in overcoming an obstacle, and a crackling cereal offers resistance on which the breakfaster can test his powers. For a similar reason, most of us choose toast rather than bread at the morning meal.

We can learn a lot from this morning routine. It is an instinctive kind of safeguard against an unhappy day. Many of the principles involved in it can be put to good use.

## Suggestions

The day ahead of you appears chaotic. The only known resting points are your lunch and dinner, possibly the beginning and end of your workday. Unstructured tasks always are frightening. By erecting a scaffold of definite time periods devoted to specific tasks, your day acquires backbone. Its unknown elements disappear. Having such plans gives you a feeling of security. You have made yourself the master of the chaos. The day is yours in the truest sense. You arrange it and divide it to suit your own needs.

Some people can do their best work early in the morning, others late at night. Some need a long time before they can get started. Their "warming up" period is long. You may belong to the type of people who can launch immediately on any kind of activity without great preparation. If you were to take the trouble, as we suggest you do, to jot down the periods at which you are best, you may learn many very interesting facts about yourself. Everyone has certain peaks and lows throughout the day. A major factor in daily happiness is the correct management of the hours of the day so that your periods of highest efficiency will coincide with the most difficult tasks. In this way you will experience the feeling of being satisfied with yourself.

Plant signposts along the route of your day. They will provide you with symbols of achievement. "This is as far as I have gone," you can say to yourself every time you reach such a mark. The value of breaking one task into a dozen smaller ones has been proved many times. In an experiment among agricultural workers, two groups of men were set to work thinning out beets. One group worked on a plot where the plants were set out in straight, unbroken lines. The second group worked in a space exactly the same size but where red flags, placed at regular intervals, broke the plot into several small fields. These red flags gave the workers something by which to judge their progress. Those who worked on the flag-studded plot actually produced 32 per cent more during the trial period than did the other group.

There are many ways in which you can set up red flags to mark your own progress. You can set goals which you promise yourself to reach. As you cross out each successive goal you derive new encouragement to go on. You may enhance this feeling of achievement by rewarding yourself. Offer yourself a cigarette, candy, a few pages from that new novel, or your favorite radio program.

One sure way to feel good at the end of a day is to be convinced that you have moved forward. You are a day further today than you were yesterday. It is not always a raise in salary or a great success that is necessary to bring about this feeling of achievement and progress. Sometimes only a new insight, one new understanding of something that had remained unclear, may give you such a feeling. Nothing wears you out more than an empty day, a day on which nothing has happened. We know people who seem to be models of human culture and when we ask them what this day has meant to them, they reply: "Nothing much."

One such person came to us complaining that, although her doctor could find no physical cause, she was chronically tired. We discovered that her life was too easy. She "woke up tired" because there was nothing to which she could look forward, no enticing events to lure her interest. She felt tired because of boredom. A new plan of constructive activities kept her busy, left no time for complaints, and shortly cured her condition of constant fatigue.

A feeling of accomplishment is necessary. Then and only then has the day been your day, for you have received a reward which truly adds to your feeling of security.

We may seem to contradict what was said above if we add that occasional lack of planning is also necessary for daily happiness. Actually, both forms of advice go together. To supplement your planned schedule, you need frequent periods of unplanned enjoyments. Such emotional dividends will help you to endure irritating incidents that are sometimes unavoidable during the course of a day. Experiments have proved that voluntary periods of spontaneous activity increase one's work efficiency.

Feeling good at the end of one day provides the best assurance that you will feel good the following day. Life moves in a circle. Once you are on the right track, you can enjoy the experiences of each day in turn, and thus achieve lasting satisfactions.

Remember that real happiness depends upon the adjustment of your everyday activities to your ideals, goals, and convictions. A man who keeps his moral principles in one compartment of his mind and his daily experience in another cannot be truly happy, for he is thus failing to accomplish the things in which he deeply believes. The unhappiest slave is the one who believes despairingly in liberty. Whatever you believe in—be it a religion, a philosophy, or a set of moral principles—strive to translate your beliefs into practical action. Even though you fail, you will feel better at the end of each day for having tried to practice your principles.

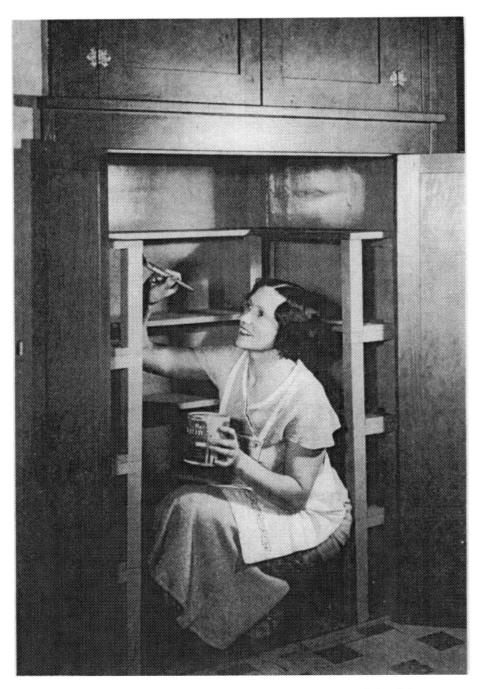

A feeling of accomplishment is necessary.

# PART II

## GETTING FUN OUT OF LIFE

People work for pleasure as well as for security and the necessities of life. When we ask, What is pleasure? we face immediately the problem of developing proper attitudes and emotions, of mental health. In our democracy, we would all like each citizen to derive the maximum enjoyment consistent with the general welfare. We try to provide abundant opportunities for getting fun out of life, but the use to which each of us puts these opportunities depends on our attitudes, beliefs, habits, and emotions. To get more fun out of life, we need to understand and apply psychological principles to everyday activities such as driving an automobile, smoking a cigarette, and listening to the radio.

The monotony of work in many of our factories and offices has increased our need for getting fun out of life. Many of our economic enterprises are conducted in a machine-like, impersonal way. Too few are the people who find most of their pleasure in their daily work. And the things we labor so hard to produce—automobiles, cigarettes, radios, and millions of other useful products—should be used effectively to add to our enjoyment of life. What, then, has the psychologist to say about these sources of pleasure?

Picnic at White Oak Canyon, Shenandoah National Park.
These people are really getting fun out of life.

# SEVEN LEAGUE BOOTS

We think of an automobile as merely a convenient means of transportation, but the psychologist's analysis proves it to be much more significant than that. It is a symbol and an expression of human desires. In wartime, it was clearly demonstrated that, apart from the inconvenience of being unable to use their cars, people missed the satisfactions and psychological advantages which a car provides.

The significance of a car is especially apparent in the United States, where, in fact, a man who does not own a car feels out of place, embarrassed, and at a great disadvantage in his efforts to gain social prestige and enjoyable associations. This over-evaluation may be traced back to early pioneer days when a horse and wagon were essential equipment. The settler needed them in order to earn his livelihood. The rifle had similar utility and importance in those days. In a sense, the automobile is our modern social equivalent of the horse, the wagon, and the rifle of the pioneers. Even where a car may no longer be needed as a means of transportation, there is considerable psychological value in owning one.

When young men of today dream about piloting an airplane, they display a definite reaching out toward a psycho-

logical goal or ambition which they expect to achieve. Nobody has to fly a plane in order to reach his destination
within a reasonable time. What, then, is the psychological
need which such means of transportation fulfill? To answer
this question, we completed several comprehensive surveys
and arrived at the following conclusions.

### Cars Are Milestones in Life

There is a close relationship between car history and life
history. All dates referring to car ownership stand out in
the owner's mind. People recall with amazing accuracy the
dates of their car purchases. Since it is true that we retain
thus vividly in our memories only those experiences that
seem important to us, our ownership must be one such experience. In fact, cars are milestones in human life, as indicated by remarks such as: "I never realized that I actually
lived my life in terms of cars." An elderly business man said,
at the end of an interview: "Is it possible? Does a man really
own so many cars in his life?" The same point is clearly
brought out in this quotation from another interview: "There
is something about cars. . . . I've owned cars since I was
eighteen years old. I can remember incidents in my life
connected with cars. Somehow, the different cars I have
had represent different periods in my life." Admitting that
cars are psychologically important in life, we may ask *why*
they are important. What does a car really mean to the individual?

### Driving Is a Symbol of Life

Tell us how a man drives, and we will tell you what kind
of man he is. This assertion is supported by adequate evidence
in our case histories.

An individual's life span may be divided into two major

periods. In the first period, that of immaturity and youth, attention is centered in immediate pleasures and aims. In the second period, usually beginning around the age of thirty-five, we become interested primarily in efficiency—in getting things done properly and most effectively. Our efforts are then directed toward specific objectives, whereas they had formerly been rather vague and diffused.

These two major periods of life are reflected distinctly in our attitudes toward cars. In the early years, a car serves mainly to satisfy our immediate desires. It is an instrument of pleasure. Later on, the desire for efficiency becomes more important. As we grow older we change not only our attitude toward cars but our driving habits as well.

## Speed

For instance, speeding, and overcoming obstacles to speeding, appeal strongly to young people. Here are two typical comments: "I enjoy the sensation of speeding up a hill and coming down again. I like the feeling of the wind rushing past."—"I like to step on the gas and watch the scenery shoot by. I like to ride in an open car and feel the wind in my hair." These first experiences of young drivers satisfy the intense desire of youth for self-assertion.

## Control

Control—the ability to make a powerful machine obey our commands — provides another source of gratification and helps to build the ego of youth. An eighteen-year-old student admitted: "I like the smooth sensation of power and the easy glide of the car. I get a feeling of swift motion. I enjoy a feeling of control over a dangerous machine." A clerk in his early thirties commented: "As a matter of fact, I would rather drive a car than fly an airplane. The avoidance of obstacles,

Driving satisfies the desire of youth for self-assertion.

the maneuvering, that's what I like. Absolute control." And a woman of thirty explained: "I like driving very much. Could drive all day. I like handling a car, steering, avoiding obstacles and missing them."

Evidently the desire for speed is strongest among the younger drivers. The older group gets most satisfaction from the feeling of power or control.

## Efficiency

Interest in efficiency is characteristic of the mature person. A careful driver of forty described his changing interest in this way: "Before I got married, I liked to impress my friends with how far I drove and in how many hours, but not now any more—that is kind of kid stuff. I have no feeling of hurrying. You get there twenty minutes later. You just sit there, anyway, if you get there earlier. I enjoy going, and why should I wish to get there quicker?" Driving becomes routine, a self-evident necessity: "A car is a part of my life. It is just as important to own a car as washing my teeth . . . It is an important part of living," said one of the older persons interviewed.

## Safety

When the individual marries and has a family, he starts thinking seriously about safety in driving. An advertising man of forty-eight explained this as follows: "My psychology has changed since I have two children and a wife. Sometimes I have to drive fast, but I put special safety catches on the back door, which works from the outside, because I always have the feeling—'God, if that door should open, with the children playing around in the back seats.' I'll probably get those special tires next time, to be safer. My psychology is changed in an automobile, because of my family."

## Comfort

As people grow older, they think more about comfort, though the exact age when comfort becomes a predominant factor varies considerably with the individual. Here are two comments by men of fifty-five and fifty-eight, respectively: "I have a sense of security in a car. She does everything she is asked to do. You don't think when you drive. It is just mechanical. I can hardly stay awake." "I don't suppose I can drive as well as I should be able to, because my eyes have always been bad, but I do enjoy a ride once in a while—cars are so comfortable."

Driving is not only a symbol of life but also a manifestation of the individual's personality.

## The Psychology of the First Car

"Do you remember when . . . ?" brings forth many rich and vivid reminiscences about one's first car. People love to talk about their cars, and they remember most enthusiastically their first car. If we understand the psychology associated with his first car, we shall better appreciate just what a car means to the individual owner.

### A SYMBOL OF OWNERSHIP

To own property is a basic human goal. Ownership seems to extend our personality so that we feel more powerful and our sense of importance expands. An old-time driver explained to us how his first car gave him a new pride of ownership: "Oh, do I remember that first car! Of course, it was a piece of junk—but still, it was my car!"

### A SYMBOL OF INDEPENDENCE

The first car is a symbol of newly won independence, of being grown up, of breaking away from family ties, of exploration and freedom. These feelings are characteristics of the age period when most people buy their first cars: from eighteen to twenty-four. Obstacles and challenges are welcome. Family life is considered too stable, dull, and safe to be very interesting. "I want to prove that I can be independent, can stand on my own feet," is the underlying thought. As one respondent summed it up: "The world is so big, and just invites me to explore it."

### SENTIMENTAL ATTACHMENT

Subsequent cars never provide so much fun as the first car; and the period from eighteen to twenty-four is one of the most pleasant in our lives. People remember their first cars with special pleasure. One car-owner remarked: "In spite of all defects, no other car has ever been like it. . . ." Our first car, moreover, is usually owned during a time of courtship and romance, so that many rich memories are associated with it. People keep their first cars much longer than necessary; their sentimental attachment to them is so great that few owners give them up without a keen feeling of regret. This comment is typical: "You get sort of fond of a car when you have to do so much for it—look after it, just like a sick child. I held the car a couple of years longer than I needed to. I could afford a new one, but I was sort of attached to my 'good old car.'" Another driver expressed his sentimental attachment thus: "I hung onto that car until the bitter end." People compare the loss of their first car with the loss of a faithful dog.

### FIRST USED CAR AND FIRST NEW CAR

The majority of first cars are used ones. Most people, because they have had trouble with their first used car, generally expect too much of their first new car. Actual experience with the first new car can never reach the heights expected of it, but nevertheless disappointment is particularly bitter if the owner experiences trouble with it: "Finally, I got a new car, and after all the troubles I had had with used cars, I thought it would be something marvelous. But it didn't take very long until I had the first troubles. Then I really lost all faith in human nature. Then I bought a Buick, primarily because I figured that certainly nothing could happen to this car."

Our car preferences may depend on experiences with a first used car, as shown by these comments: "I once had a bad carburetor in a Pontiac. Whenever, later on, a Pontiac salesman would approach me, my first question automatically would be about the carburetor—although I knew exactly that I had that bad experience only because I had a second-hand car. But still, I couldn't get rid of the thought, and I shall probably never again buy a Pontiac." Here, on the other hand, is a favorable comment on "the first car": "Buick represents for me one of the oldest names—must be a good solid product. I told you, when I bought my first car, it was a Buick—she was ten years old already—I drove it for about one and a half years and even my meddling could not kill it. It was really solid, and as such it has left a feeling in me. Some day, when I can afford it, I would like to own a Buick again."

*The Influence of Convertibles*

Most young people dream of their first car as a convertible. The desire for perennial youth is symbolized in convertible models. Youngsters are attracted to a make by its convertibles, though practical considerations, such as price and utility, usually induce purchasers to settle on a closed model of the same make of car. Here is a typical rationalization of car preference: "The reason that I have a convertible is that they have leather seats, and, with children in the family, they can stand up and spill stuff on them—get candy all over them. All you have to do is to wipe it off, whereas the regular upholstery looks like the devil when it gets spotted up, which it sometimes does." A more emotional driver exclaimed: "I hate those sedans! I think that nice feeling of just driving and driving you lose in sedans, because they are covered. Too bad my wife doesn't like a convertible. Maybe I'll finally overcome all objections and get an open car next year." People visiting a show room invariably inspect the convertible models first of all. Often, they end up by buying another model, but they are loth to leave the convertible. They even stop outside, after the transaction, to look back wistfully at the convertible that they did not buy.

They end up by buying another model.

*Ewing Galloway*

*The Car Ideal*

When the average man thinks or talks about his car, his description of it is colored by a psychological aura, by his car ideal. Nearly everyone has a car ideal, which is generally stated in vivid language, such as: "I'd give my right eye for one of those real streamlined cars that are set way down low and purr and roar when you step on the gas." Our car ideal is formed very early in life. It is built up as a result of many influences. Every car we see, every ride we take, every advertisement we read, adds new bricks to the foundations of our car ideal. The following comments illustrate this point: "Sometimes I do wonder if it isn't possible to have one of those big cars, and I sit up half the night with pencil and pad and figure, trying to dope out a way it could be financed without taking too much out of my pocket. But I always come to the final conclusion that it can't be done. I'm pretty good on figures, but why try to do the impossible? If I got a real good car, I'd get a Chrysler or a LaSalle. In a lot of ways, it fits in with what I have always had in mind that a car should be. It's streamlined, and it's fast from what I hear." And another person said, very definitely: "Well, I'd like a light blue convertible, with nice comfortable upholstery, and a cigarette lighter. The car has to have a fancy horn—the old single toot is out of style." Still another remarked, just as definitely: "My ideal car would be a blue or gray roadster, nice and streamlined and of good solid construction."

We asked unmarried girls what cars they thought their future husbands should have. Their answers were very similar to those above. One typist replied: "I'd like a smart-looking automobile. I would look for the body first of all and, of course, the comfort inside. I would not get a car unless it was smart-looking—a sport model—what I call something smart is the body of Packard. If I could afford it, that

would be my ideal car. It has a lot of dash to it. Richness—
that's exactly what I mean." How far these young women
will go towards carrying out their car ideal when they finally
buy a car, is hard to say. They may have to compromise, or
new influences may modify their ideal, but some of the attributes of their car ideal will undoubtedly persist, and take
shape in reality.

The Second World War probably changed the car ideal
of many people. In the future, they may expect better performance. Subconsciously, they will compare the automobile
to the airplane. As our surveys indicate, they will also better
appreciate factors of utility and durability. War taught many
of us to consider the intrinsic quality of a product as contrasted with its superficial appearance.

### Cars Have "Personality"

Personality is a complicated psychological structure composed of many elements. We have only a vague idea as to
the personality of an individual whom we do not know.
If we meet him, however, his personality becomes meaningful and real to us. We can apply the same idea to our analysis
of the psychology of cars. As we gain more experience with a
car, we ascribe so-called "traits of personality" to it.

Handling the steering wheel provides our closest contact
with a car. One of our respondents described his reactions
as follows: "I get the feeling of a car through the steering
wheel. I turn it with one finger and sometimes I like to handle the wheel like this—with flat hands. I find myself doing
it unconsciously." And here is the same thought expressed
differently by another: "My present car has a very large
wheel which is very thin. That gives me the feeling of ele-
gance and sleekness. It has a very definite action of its own.
She flips back like a spring and comes around on her own.

Lots of temperament. I think that when I am driving, myself, the expert manipulation of that wheel, the delicacy of the touch, gives me a certain unconscious satisfaction. It is like a horse—the fine touch, the expertness of the touch."

Excerpts from our interviews show how deeply people feel attached to their cars. Here are several typical examples: "My car is more of a companion to me than I figured one could be."—"I felt as though the car really fitted me—we belonged together. I felt at home in it, just like in a house." —"Whenever I trade a car in, I have the feeling of losing a friend."

People point proudly to advertisements in magazines and to billboards displaying their cars, and say, "That's my car!" just as if their own names were on display. One driver said: "When you're driving a Plymouth and see a big sign with the name Plymouth, it gives you a feeling of relationship and identification." Another commented: "We bought a Dodge, but it could not be delivered right away. We had to wait several weeks . . . but our car was in the window of the dealer. We made it a regular family excursion and even took our friends along and showed them 'our car' in the window."

*Symbols of Success*

Automobile manufacturers have made their product an integral part of our American social structure. Social approval has become a principal psychological factor in the sale of cars. In all walks of life, the automobile has become a symbol of success.

People want to be envied, looked up to, conspicuously successful. As one owner rather sheepishly admitted: "I'm ashamed to say it, but I bought a new car because I actually wanted to look successful. There really wasn't anything wrong with my old car." A housewife in her middle forties expressed her feeling of superiority as follows: "You are really only half a person without a nice car. Every owner feels himself entitled to look down upon the other drivers with a shabbier car." And a young farmer testified: ". . . but this new Plymouth, she just perks right up and shoots ahead. I like to pass cars on the road. It always makes me feel that I am somebody, and that the others have got an old hack that never could run an inch. Of course, I'm smart enough to realize that that is foolish, but that's the way I feel about it, anyway."

All such reactions really signify a type of social competition. We compare ourselves with other people, our cars with theirs, and we feel superior if we can assure ourselves that we are "better off." Wherever people gather, some of them begin to compare their cars. If they were frank, they might admit a secret hope that they would be able to depreciate other cars as compared with their own. The same motive impels people to inquire how much money others earn, in order that they may say to themselves, "I am not so badly off, after all."

We not only compare our present condition with that of our associates but also enjoy memories of ways in which we were able to "keep up with the Joneses." The following case, told us by a person interviewed, is typical of many others: "I have very rich relatives, and I also competed a little with them. As a very young man, I came to the home of my uncle. He didn't want me to go to college. His idea was to take me into his business. However, I left his house, studied under very difficult circumstances, and then, when I was graduated, it was my ambition to prove to my uncle that one can also become rich as a physician, not only as a businessman. One of the first indications of being well off is the ownership of a car. When I got my first shabby Ford, he laughed at me, but it didn't take me long before I got the same make of car he had. And I felt completely happy about it only because I knew it would aggravate him."

Above all, we fear the loss of social prestige. If we change from an expensive car to a cheaper model, we feel as if we had lowered our whole standard of living. Just to keep up appearances, people buy costly automobiles even when they can no longer afford them. A psychological analysis of our case histories reveals that many people experience a fear that they may somehow be punished for this extravagance. Witness such comments as: "I should not have had that car in the first place. I was overstepping the balance of my income."—"At that time I had my choice between a Pontiac and a very nice Studebaker. But, frankly speaking, I was frightened that my boss would think that I was making too much money when I could drive a Studebaker. So I made up my mind and bought the Pontiac."—"No one else near us had a car. Most everyone had horses. Some folks were kinda sore at us gettin' a car. There was talk about us makin' lots of money. We weren't but we were the kind of family that always likes to be up on the latest things. When the first radio came out, I remember my father was right there, Johnny-on-the-spot, to get one."

The influence of social approval can sometimes overshadow that of technical quality and engineering perfection. A car may be superb in performance, but, if it has been rejected by public opinion, no amount of advertising will sell that car. The following comment is typical of many: "Willys has something very appealing about its streamlining. . . . I remember, though, a lot of us laughed when it first came out. They were exceptionally good on the road, but who wants a car that people laugh at—no matter how good it is supposed to be?"

We discovered too, that when a certain income level has been reached, an interesting reversal takes place. People then start to buy cheaper cars. But their motive is the same: "Keeping up with the standard of your class." They show off by not showing off. Such people say, "I am so rich, or so well established, that I just don't have to care about appearances any more." Obviously, this group includes only a small minority of the population.

As we probe deeper into our analysis of the automobile as a symbol of success, we find certain other and more subtle psychological influences.

To the average car owner, for instance, each motor trip symbolizes success. The ability to start out, overcome obstacles, and arrive safely at his destination gives the owner a feeling of successful achievement. Our lives are made up of these minor successes. Each trip represents a dual accomplishment of car and driver. "I enjoy driving very much," said one of our respondents. "It is almost a passion. A feeling of power. It gives me a sense of freedom, a sense of accomplishment." Another put it this way: "My wife used to say, 'That Plymouth certainly gets us there and back.'"

All of us strive to get ahead. We enjoy the appearance of superiority. A car enhances our feeling of dominance, of superiority, of power. Many people, after a setback in their everyday affairs, get into their cars and drive off, usually at high speed. They are seeking to restore their shaken self-confidence. Through driving, they develop their personality. They reëstablish their self-confidence in much the same way in which a youngster builds self-assurance by driving his first car. One of our women respondents reported: "To me, driving is a restful thing, even in heavy traffic, even in jams. It takes me away from other things which might be bothering me. In other words, driving is a relief."

Modern man is impatient. He cannot wait. A car provides an antidote for impatience. Furthermore, driving takes us out of a rut. Also, it compensates to some extent for lack of achievement. We need successes, and we are impatient for them. "I like to drive very fast," confessed one respondent. "There is a certain feeling of power—the ability to direct the thing and make it go. The feeling of being able to control something. Around here in New York, it is not much pleasure; in the Middle West, where there's a lot more room, you can drive as fast as you like." Everyone has a desire for quick success. When we go to the motion pictures, we share vicariously in the exploits of the hero, who may be a newsboy one minute and a millionaire the next. The automobile symbolizes this widespread interest in quick success, as for example, when we boast: "I got there in two hours flat."

The urge to destroy and the fear of death are deep in what Freud called our "subconscious." Expressions like "Give it to 'em" and "Step on it" reflect the satisfaction we derive from a feeling of power. The psychologist interprets these reactions as based on a submerged desire for aggression or sadism.

The expression "I just missed that truck by inches" reflects an interest in "playing with danger." How often do we hear a motorist say, "Well, I brought you home safely, didn't I?" The driver thus becomes a hero, a savior, a protector. Lives have been entrusted to his keeping, and he brought everybody through without a scratch. All this he attributes to his driving skills. This attitude is common, so it is not at all surprising to find that almost everyone considers himself a good driver.

Our analysis shows that the automobile is a modern symbol of achievement and prestige. But, more than that, we have indicated the process whereby such products are used as a

{ 84 }

means of personal progress and success. Driving is part of the universal search for social security in a society wherein security can be attained through facing danger, overcoming obstacles, and coping with ever-changing situations. In the early days, the automobile was condemned as an instrument of injury and death. Properly controlled, however, it enriches our feeling of being "at home in the world." In fact, the automobile reflects not only the progress of science and technology but also the psychological character of our modern communities. Our people, young and old, prize highly the feeling of being up-to-date, efficient, and free to go when and where they please. In purchasing and using automobiles, they have showed themselves to be self-confident, competitive, sentimental, impatient. Perhaps this is why they own more than two thirds of the automobiles in the world and get more comfort and fun out of life.

An auto enriches our feeling of being at home in the world.

*Ewing Galloway*

# Why do we smoke Cigarettes?

None of the much flaunted appeals of cigarette advertisers, such as superior taste and mildness, induces us to become smokers or to choose one brand in preference to another. Despite the emphasis put on such qualities by advertisers, they are minor considerations. This is one of the first facts we discovered when we asked several hundred people, from all walks of life, why they liked to smoke cigarettes. Smoking is as much a psychological pleasure as it is a physiological satisfaction. As one of our respondents explained: "It is not the taste that counts. It's that sense of satisfaction you get from a cigarette that you can't get from anything else."

## Smoking is Fun

What is the nature of this psychological pleasure? It can be traced to the universal desire for self-expression. None of us ever completely outgrows his childhood. We are constantly hunting for the carefree enjoyment we knew as children. As we grew older, we had to subordinate our pleasures to work and to the necessity for unceasing effort. Smoking, for many of us, then, became a substitute for our early habit of following the whims of the moment; it becomes a legitimate excuse for interrupting work and snatching a moment of pleasure. "You sometimes get tired of working intensely," said an accountant whom we interviewed, "and if you sit back for the length of a cigarette, you feel much fresher afterwards. It's a peculiar thing, but I wouldn't think of just sitting back without a cigarette. I guess a cigarette somehow gives me a good excuse."

### Smoking is a Reward

Most of us are hungry for rewards. We want to be patted on the back. A cigarette is a reward that we can give ourselves as often as we wish. When we have done anything well, for instance, we can congratulate ourselves with a cigarette, which certifies, in effect, that we have been "good boys." We can promise ourselves: "When I have finished this piece of work, when I have written the last page of my report, I'll deserve a little fun. I'll have a cigarette."

The first and the last cigarette in the day are especially significant rewards. The first one, smoked right after breakfast, is a sort of anticipated recompense. The smoker has work to do, and he eases himself into the day's activities as pleasantly as possible. He gives himself a little consolation prize in advance, and at the same time manages to postpone the evil hour when he must begin his hard day's work. The last cigarette of the day is like "closing a door." It is something quite definite. One smoker explained: "I nearly always smoke a cigarette before going to bed. That finishes the day. I usually turn the light out after I have smoked the last cigarette, and then turn over to sleep."

Smoking is often merely a conditioned reflex. Certain situations, such as coming out of the subway, beginning and ending work, voluntary and involuntary interruptions of work, feelings of hunger, and many others regulate the timetable of smoking. Often a smoker may not even want a cigarette particularly, but he will see someone else take one and then he feels that he must have one, too.

While to many people smoking is fun, and a reward in itself, it more often accompanies other pleasures. At meals, a cigarette is somewhat like another course. In general, smoking introduces a holiday spirit into everyday living. It rounds out other forms of enjoyment and makes them one hundred per cent satisfactory.

## Smoking is Oral Pleasure

As we have said, to explain the pleasure derived from smoking as taste experience alone, is not sufficient. For one thing, such an explanation leaves out the powerful erotic sensitivity of the oral zone. Oral pleasure is just as funda-

Smoking rounds out other forms of enjoyment.

mental as sexuality and hunger. It functions with full strength from earliest childhood. There is a direct connection between thumbsucking and smoking. "In school I always used to chew a pencil or a pen," said a journalist, in reply to our questions. "You should have seen the collection I had. They used to be chewed to bits. Whenever I try to stop smoking for a while, I get something to chew on, either a pipe or a menthol cigarette. You just stick it in your mouth and keep on sucking. And I also chew a lot of gum when I want to cut down on smoking. . . ."

The satisfied expression on a smoker's face when he inhales the smoke is ample proof of his sensuous thrill. The immense power of the yearning for a cigarette, especially after an enforced abstinence, is acknowledged by habitual smokers. One of our respondents said: "When you don't get a cigarette for a long time and you are kind of on pins, the first drag goes right down to your heels."

## The Cigarette—A Modern Hourglass

Frequently the burning down of a cigarette functions psychologically as a time indicator. A smoker waiting for someone who is late says to himself, "Now I'll smoke one more cigarette, and then I am off." One person explained, "It is much easier to watch a cigarette get smaller and smaller than to keep watching a clock and look at the hands dragging along."

In some countries, the farmers report distances in terms of the number of pipes, as, for example, "It's about three pipes from here to Smithtown."

A cigarette not only measures time, but also seems to make time pass more rapidly. That is why waiting periods almost automatically stimulate the desire to smoke. But a deeper explanation of this function of smoking is based on the fact that smoking is *ersatz activity*. Impatience is a common feature of our times, but there are many situations which *compel* us to be patient. When we are in a hurry, and yet have to wait, a cigarette gives us something to do during that trying interval. The experience of wanting to act, but being unable to do so, is very unpleasant and may even, in extreme cases, cause attacks of nervous anxiety. Cigarettes may then have a psychotherapeutic effect. This helps to explain why soldiers, waiting for the signal to attack, sometimes value a cigarette more than food.

### *"With a Cigarette I Am Not Alone"*

Frequently, our respondents remarked that smoking cigarettes is like being with a friend. Said one, "When I lean back and light my cigarette and see the glow in the dark, I am not alone any more . . ." In one sense, a cigarette seems to be something alive. When it is lighted it appears to be awakened, brought to life. In a French moving picture (*Daybreak*) the hunted criminal, played by Jean Gabin, holds out as long as he has his cigarettes. He barricades himself against the police and stands siege courageously for some time—until his last cigarette is gone. Then he gives up.

The companionable character of cigarettes is also reflected in the fact that they help us make friends. In many ways, smoking has the same effect as drinking has. It helps to break down social barriers. Two smokers out on a date light up a cigarette as soon as they get into their car. "It's just the right start for an evening," they say. Immediately they feel at ease, for they have found an interest they both share.

We could report many true anecdotes to illustrate how cigarettes bring people together. One such story was related by a middle-aged lady: "A long time ago, on a steamer, there was a boy I was quite eager to meet . . . but there was no one to introduce us. . . . The second day out, he was sitting at a table right next to me, and I was puffing away at my cigarette. The ashes on my cigarette were getting longer and longer, and I had no ash tray. Suddenly he jumped up and brought me one. That's how the whole thing started. We are still happily married."

### "I Like to Watch the Smoke"

In mythology and religion, smoke is full of meaning. Its floating intangibility and unreal character have made it possible for imaginative man to see therein mystery and magic. Even for us moderns, smoke has a strong fascination. To the cigarette smoker, the clouds he puffs out seem to represent a part of himself. Just as most people like to watch their own breath on cold winter days, so they like to watch cigarette smoke, which similarly makes one's breath visible. This explains the emotional attitudes of many toward smoke. "Smoke is fascinating," said one of the people we interviewed. "I like to watch the smoke. On a rainy day, I sort of lie in a haze in the middle of the room and let my thoughts wander while I smoke and wonder where the smoke goes."

The desire to make things is deep-rooted—and smoke is manufactured by the smoker himself. Smoking provides satisfaction because it is a playful, creative activity. This fact was well stated by one cigarette devotee as follows: "It's a fascinating thing to watch the smoke take shape. The smoke, like clouds, can form different shapes. . . . You like to sit back and blow rings and then blow another ring through the first ones. You are perfectly relaxed."

### "Got a Match?"

Some of the appeals of a lighted cigarette derive from the appeals of fire in general. Fire is the symbol of life, and the idea of fire is surrounded by much superstition. In this connection, it is interesting to note that traces of superstition can be seen in the smoking habits of modern man. For instance some people never will light three cigarettes on one match. It is said that this superstition is based on experiences during World War I. As three soldiers were lighting up, the third man was hit when the light of a match flared up for the last time. Our custom of lighting another smoker's cigarette for him may sometimes have an erotic significance, or it may serve as a friendly gesture. Match and cigarette are contact points.

## Smoking Memories

Certain moments in our lives are closely linked with cigarettes. These situations often leave on people's memories an important imprint never to be forgotten. Here is such an occasion, described by an office clerk of twenty-one. ". . . I can remember the moments when I returned home—no matter how late—after having been out with a girl on a Saturday night. Before going to bed, I'd sit on the fire escape for a while and enjoy a smoke. I'd turn around so that I could see the smoke going up. At the same time, the windows would be bright with lights on the other side of the courtyard. I would watch what the people were doing. I would sit, and watch, and think about what my girl and I had talked about and what a nice time we had had together. Then I'd throw the cigarette away and go to bed. I feel these were really the most contented moments in my life. . . ."

"I remember one time we were in North Africa on a trip and it was evening," said one of our respondents, a nurse about twenty-seven years of age. "During the day, I had noticed that there was a lovely spot to sit, across the way from the hotel where we were staying. I went there at night, and sat looking at the stars and the tall cypresses illuminated against the night sky. I was far away in my thoughts. I was thinking of God and the beautiful world he had made. The smoke from my cigarette rose slowly into the sky. I was alone, and at the same time I was a part of all the world around me. . . ."

*Smoking Mannerisms*

Usually the way we smoke is characteristic of our whole personality. The mannerisms of smokers are innumerable. Some people always have cigarettes drooping from their mouths. Others let the cigarette jump up and down in their mouths while they are talking. Men sometimes complain about the way women smoke: "A lot of women blow out the smoke with a gust of wind, right into your face. They just puff it at you." Some men, when they want to appear to be aggressive, hold their cigarettes with thumb and forefinger so that the glowing end shows toward the palm of the hand.

Often smokers will assume a pose, because they have found that it fits their personality best, or at least they think so. A not too modest glamor girl revealed to us some of her "smoking secrets": "I think it looks so much better to smoke with a holder. I studied that very carefully. Don't you think I'm somewhat of a Latin type? It all really depends on what type you are. . . . I always have holders that are long and dark. I think a long holder is somewhat like a big hat: it's alluring and 'don't dare to come close' at the same time."

While every smoker has to go through the motions of lighting and inhaling the smoke, the way in which these acts are carried out varies according to his mood. The nervous smoker has a faster smoking tempo than the relaxed one. The angry smoker blows the smoke in an aggressive way, almost as if he were trying to blow somebody down. A smoker who is about to ask for a raise in salary will press his lips tightly around the cigarette as if to gain courage by holding it that way.

### "Smoking Helps Me Think"

The mind can concentrate best when all outside stimuli have been excluded. Smoking literally provides a sort of "smoke screen" that helps to shut out distractions. This explains why many people who were interviewed reported that they cannot think or write without a cigarette. They argued that moderate smoking may even stimulate mental alertness. It gives us a focal point for our attention. It also gives our hands something to do; otherwise they might make us self-conscious and interfere with mental activity. On the other hand, our respondents admit that smoking too much may reduce their efficiency.

### Cigarettes Help Us to Relax

One shortcoming of our modern culture is the universal lack of adequate relaxation. Many of us not only do not know how to relax, but do not take time to learn. Smoking helps us to relax because, like music, it is rhythmic. Smoking gives us a legitimate excuse to linger a little longer after meals, to stop work for a few minutes, to sit at home without doing anything that requires effort. Here is a nostalgic comment contributed by a strong defender of smoking: "After a long day's work, to get home and sit in a chair and stretch my legs 'way out, and then to sit back and just smoke a cigarette and think of nothing, just blow the smoke in the air —that's what I like to do when I have had a pretty tough day." The restful effect of moderate smoking explains why people working under great stress use more tobacco.

### "I Blow My Troubles Away"

In times of high tension, cigarettes provide relief, as indicated by the following typical comments of one of our respondents: "When I have a problem, and it comes back and back, warningly saying, 'Well, what are you going to do about this?' a cigarette almost acts like a consolation. Somehow it relieves the pressure on my chest. The feeling of relief is almost like what you feel in your chest after you have cried because something has hurt you very much. Relaxing is not the right kind of word for that feeling. It is like having been in a stuffy room for a long time and at last getting out for a deep breath of air." That man's explanation comes very close to stating the scientific reason why smoking brings relief. Worry, anxiety, depress us not only psychologically but also physiologically. When a person feels depressed, the rhythm of his breathing becomes upset. A short and shallow breath creates a heavy feeling in the chest. Smoking may relieve mental depression by forcing a rhythmic expansion of the breast and thus restoring the normal pace of breathing. The "weight on the chest" is removed.

This connection between smoking and respiration accounts for the common expression, "Smoking helps us to let off steam." When we are enraged, we breathe heavily. Smoking makes us breathe more steadily, and thus calms us down.

### Cigarette Taste Has to Be Acquired

Most people like the smell of tobacco but dislike the taste of a cigarette. Frequently we were reminded that "a cigarette never tastes as good as it smells." One usually very much dislikes his first cigarette. Taste for cigarettes must be acquired slowly. And whenever a smoker tries out a new brand, with a slightly different taste, he finds that he has to repeat this process of becoming accustomed to the taste. Often smokers who say they do not like the taste of certain brands really mean that they are not accustomed to it. Few advertisers of cigarettes realize that it takes time for a smoker to change his taste habits. No matter how pleasant the taste qualities of a brand may seem to be, at first the unaccustomed taste will be disliked. One of our respondents made the following interesting comment on this point: "I went to Bulgaria once and was forced to smoke Bulgarian cigarettes. I tried one brand after another till I had gone through five brands. Finally, the sixth brand seemed to be perfect. I discovered much later that any of the other brands might have become my preferred brand if only I had tried it in the sixth place. It just took me that long to learn to appreciate Bulgarian tobacco."

Tobacco auctioneer chanting his bids.

## How Many a Day?

Despite all the millions spent on comparing the potentially harmful effects of different brands of cigarettes, our respondents seemed very little concerned about this matter. But all of them, even those who do not smoke excessively, worry about the quantities they smoke. Scientific and medical studies on the physiological effects of smoking provide a confused picture: Some conclude that smoking is harmful; others deny it. This same confusion prevails among smokers themselves. Nevertheless, all of them worry about smoking too many cigarettes, as shown by the fact that nearly everyone has tried, at one time or another, to "cut down on" smoking. "I'll tell you something I do," one smoker confided. "I give up smoking cigarettes every year for one month, and I say to myself that I'll prove to myself I can still do without them." Periodic abstemiousness of this kind indicates an underlying feeling of guilt. Such individuals really think that constant smoking is not only harmful, but also a bit immoral. Efforts to reduce the amount of smoking signify a willingness to sacrifice pleasure in order to assuage their feeling of guilt.

The mind has a powerful influence on the body, and may produce symptoms of physical illness. Guilt feelings may cause harmful physical effects not at all caused by the cigarettes used, which may be extremely mild. Such guilt feelings alone may be the real cause of the injurious consequences.

## The First Cigarette

Much of this guilt feeling can be traced directly to one's first cigarette, which the older generation remember as a forbidden and sinful thing. Their fathers considered the habit an educational problem, whereas many parents nowadays have adopted a "modern" attitude toward smoking.

Here is what one such father said: "I told my son I thought he was a little young . . . He is seventeen. It might not do him any harm to wait another year or two. Then I remembered my own first cigarette and what awful stuff I had to smoke in secret. In a way, my son is lucky to be able to start with a good cigarette without running the danger of ruining his health. I gave him a pack of the brand I smoke."

Most of us remember vividly the first cigarette we smoked. "I certainly remember my first cigarette," said one of our respondents. "We were a bunch of boys on our way to a football game. I had trouble lighting my cigarette, and at that moment a man passed by and yelled at me: 'Throw that cigarette away, you rascal!' I was so shocked and frightened that I obeyed his command without hesitation. But only a few minutes later, I lighted another one just to demonstrate to myself that I was not afraid."

### "No, Thanks, I'll Smoke My Own"

This is the reply of most smokers when they are offered a brand different from their own. Brand loyalty among smokers is strong and persistent. Individuals smoke one brand consistently, so that they become identified with it. A guest who discovers that his host smokes the same brand considers this a personal flattery. If a young lady changes to the brand of an admirer, he understands that he has surely made an impression. Here is the experience of one young man, and his interpretation of it: "I was very fond of a girl. She was giving a farewell party before leaving the country. I didn't have any idea how I stood in her affection. The only clue was that at her party she had my brand of cigarettes. I always felt that that was in deference to me." "My brand" has a special significance, as if it were a part of the smoker's credo and personality.

## A Package of Pleasure

A new pack of cigarettes gives one a pleasant feeling. A full, firm pack in the hand signifies that one is provided for, and gives satisfaction, whereas an almost empty pack creates a feeling of want and gives a decidedly unpleasant impression. The empty pack gives us a feeling of real frustration and deprivation.

During the seventeenth century, religious leaders and statesmen in many countries condemned the use of tobacco. Smokers were excommunicated by the Church and some of them were actually condemned to death and executed. But the habit of smoking spread rapidly all over the world. The psychological pleasures derived proved much more powerful than religious, moral, and legal persuasions. As in the case of the prohibition experiment in the United States, repressive measures seem to have aroused a spirit of popular rebellion and helped to increase the use of tobacco.

If we consider all the pleasure and advantages provided, in a most democratic and international fashion, by this little white paper roll, we shall understand why it is difficult to destroy its power by means of warnings, threats, or preachings. This pleasure miracle has so much to offer that we can safely predict the cigarette is here to stay. Our psychological analysis is not intended as a eulogy of the habit of smoking, but rather as an objective report on why people smoke cigarettes. Perhaps this will seem more convincing if we reveal a personal secret: We ourselves do not smoke at all. We may be missing a great deal.

# What radio can do for us..

After a hard day at the office, Mr. Jones comes home tired. He puts on a pair of slippers, slides into his favorite armchair, reaches for his pipe or his cigarettes, and turns on the radio. His routine is like that of millions of other American men, irrespective of class or group, education, or occupation. Mrs. Jones, who stays at home all day, follows a somewhat different routine. Many women at home turn on the radio as soon as their husbands have gone to work and the children have been sent off to school. The children, too, have their own routine. They have their programs and their hours during which they reign supreme over the dials and the knobs. Habits and tastes in radio listening may vary among different groups, but in all cases there must be some universal psychological reason why we all listen to the radio.

"Why do you listen to the radio?" our research workers asked hundreds of people. The answers we received were inadequate. Some people replied that they listened for fun, for relaxation, or for a chance to learn about current events. Others said they wished to hear the weather reports and the news. Some stated that they liked a particular performer or the gags of a favorite comedian. There were many such explanations, and at first they all sounded convincing. But, as we listened to these responses, we wondered, Is there not something more fundamental that attracts people to the radio? What part does radio listening play in their lives? We suspected that radio has a far-reaching influence on the life of the individual, an influence of which he is not generally aware. We had noted that, whenever a radio character well known to the listening public plays the role of a man about to be married or divorced, he receives hundreds and thousands of letters, unsolicited letters offering friendly advice, or congratulating him, or warning him of the dangers of his intended action. Yes, the radio has a firm hold on the public. On one occasion a radio station went off the air for half a day. At once, thousands of listeners wrote to describe their reactions to the dead silence of their radio sets.

As everyone knows, in Europe, during wartime, radio was an important secret instrument of the underground. Even the routine broadcasts of governments took on ominous underlying significance. During the past decade, all the main events that vitally affect the individual's life have been announced over the radio. We have come to attach great authority to official radio messages. Presidential announcements, government proclamations, and news flashes have all helped to make us think of radio as a vital instrument of communication.

To be sure, radio has been blamed for innumerable evils. It has been charged with making people neurotic, with raising their blood pressure and causing them to have bad dreams. It has been cursed for its supposedly nefarious influence on youth. But, on the other hand, it has been lauded for providing invaluable help in the war effort and for bringing encouragement to the people. Philosophers and educators have pinned their hopes on radio, and other forms of

Radio has a far-reaching influence.

mass communication, as instruments with which to help rebuild our world.

To find out what radio means in the life of the average citizen, and how the influence of radio and television programs might be improved, we interviewed individuals, conducted experiments, and observed audiences in radio and television studios. The following facts and comments summarize our main conclusions.

### Radio Offers Security

In our homes we feel secure, in a narrow sense, but we need contacts with the outside world. Radio provides such contacts admirably. Especially in times of crisis, when our feeling of insecurity is heightened by the swift and unpredictable pace of world events, radio is a means of reassurance. As one person expressed it, "I keep the radio going all day, just so I'm not alone. It cheers me up."

People in distress seek the companionship of others. Similarly, in time of great joy we seek the sympathetic understanding of other people. During the war period, the services performed by radio were universally appreciated. When the end of the war was announced over the air, radio became truly a psychological window through which the joyful reactions of all civilized people could be heard.

Radio provides security and consolation for invalids confined to their homes. "With the radio, you feel you are not alone," said one. "You know there are thousands of others listening right along with you."

Nowadays, important events occur in such rapid succession that it is extremely difficult to keep track of them. At any moment, news may be reported that can affect our lives profoundly, and we need to be informed promptly. Radio makes it possible for us to obtain essential information promptly and easily, and it helps us to keep up to date so that we can cope with the rapidly shifting problems and forces of our age. "Well, in this day and age, you've got to know what's going on while you're asleep," remarked one respondent. And another stated: "I like to listen to the morning news. I do that, although I have the newspaper in front of me. I feel I'm getting even fresher news than from the paper." In our researches, we found that most listeners consider the early morning news and the late night news especially significant. They feel this way because they need the security that comes from timely knowledge. At night, they want last-minute news so that they will know there is no danger of their failing to take any necessary action. In the morning, they want to catch up with all the events that may have occurred during the night.

## Radio Personalities

Besides providing useful knowledge, radio brings the listening audience easily into contact with interesting personalities. Our surveys show that most listeners respond to the radio performers rather than to the programs as such. The average listener is well acquainted with a score or more of national performers.

Each of these performers is associated, in the listener's mind, with a type of personality. Kate Smith is accepted as representing motherly sentiment; Charlie McCarthy, sophisticated humor; Jack Benny, clownish humor. One typical comment was: "I just love my radio. My favorites are Jack Benny and Charlie McCarthy. I listen to them every Sunday. I think they are perfectly wonderful. I wouldn't ever miss them, for anything under the sun." Radio personalities have become important symbols of modern life. People traveling abroad keep in touch with home by listening to some of their favorite shows.

Our leading radio actors appeal to the listening audience because they resemble, in many ways, the so-called "average" or "typical" individual. In other words, the performers adapt themselves to their audience. At the same time, however, listeners accept the performers as representatives of the national character. The radio listener adds these famous radio friends to his intimate family circle or social group, and thus derives a feeling of increased power and security.

## Radio Teaches Techniques of Living

To what extent can radio teach listeners the techniques of successful living in the modern world? Our studies of daytime serial stories, the so-called "soap operas," may help to answer this question.

There are many different types of radio programs—quizzes, news reports, comedy shows, and so on. Of these, the radio drama and the daytime serials are most revealing to the psychologist. Daytime serials are continued stories some of which have been on the air for years. Approximately twenty million women listen to these stories every day, and reactions prove that the programs have great influence on them.

One of the most frequent comments of listeners, when asked why they like daytime serials, is, "They are so true to life." Interestingly enough, the same criterion is used by women who dislike to listen to the serials. They say they do not like the stories because they are *not* "true to life." We can safely assume, therefore, that this "true to life" quality in a story is of great psychological importance to the listener.

What do listeners really mean when they use this expression? They differ in their interpretations. Some listeners mean that the stories remind them of their own lives. Others have in mind the same idea as the naïve art critic who says that a painting is so realistic that he feels like reaching out for the objects portrayed. In the latter case, the phrase "true to life" signifies a certain esthetic evaluation as to clarity and three-dimensional reality. To say that a story is *not* true to life might mean that "things like these do not happen in real life," or it might refer to the lack of plausibility in the plot, the strangeness of dramatized events, the "untrue" characters.

But these varying definitions of "trueness to life" have one common denominator: the relationship between the life experiences depicted in the daytime serials, and the real-life experiences of the listener. What are the psychological components of this relationship?

Whenever we listen to the radio, see a moving picture, or read a book, we do so within the framework of a larger field of perception. This field varies with different types of program or subject matter. When listening to a mystery story, we react differently from the way we react when listening to a "true to life" story. Just as we apply different sets of criteria to a photograph and to a painting, so our standards of expression differ for a detective story and a sophisticated psychological novel. Said one respondent: "Listening to 'Big Sister' is like calling up an old friend to see what's going on in her life . . ." To explain how a "true to life" story may influence the listener, we must raise the question, To what extent are we living our lives by the grace of literature? By this, we mean that when we get married, for instance, some of us cannot help being reminded of a moving picture scene or of a novel in which a detailed description of a marriage ceremony has been described. Even a person who has never read accepted works of literature will have heard others tell of such experiences. His parents may have described their wedding to him. Any form of reality has its counterpart—its literary portrayal—which shows us the proper techniques for dealing with the situations of life.

*Radio Makes Life Easier*

There are certain basic differences between fictional portrayals of life and actual occurrences. Nevertheless, real life is not on an entirely different level of reality from that of fictional depiction of life situations. In everyday living, certain episodes have a much higher degree of reality than others. We may have walked along a certain street hundreds of times without ever having particularly noticed that street. One day, we return from a long trip and are more attentive than usual. Then only does the street take on a higher degree

About twenty million women listen to daytime serials.

of reality for us. It is then that we really *experience* that street for the first time.

Normally, the individual lives on a rather low level of reality. Perhaps we should say, instead, that his perceptual horizons are limited. Daytime serials and radio dramas make the listener aware of previously ignored elements of his real world, by dramatizing them in story form. Thus these dramas broaden his horizon of reality. Such serials seem to put the accent on the relatively flat world of the listener and make his field of life a structured relief. One of our respondents remarked: "I enjoy the radio because I like to find out how other people are living."

At the same time, however, listening to fictional incidents —that is, to events on a new level of reality—has several other consequences. There is. a direct relationship between levels of reality and the amount of difficulty we encounter in efforts to achieve our goals. Dreaming and fantasy take place on a low level of reality, and goals which we cannot achieve, in real life, are within easy reach in our dreams and fantasies. No matter how true to life, fiction, too, is on a lower level of reality than actual experience, and this is one reason why daytime serials are highly popular. Listeners seem to obtain assurance and comfort from stories which portray successful attempts to solve lifelike problems. Note these typical comments of our respondents: "If I see what happened in the story, it might help me if the same things happen to me."—"Some of the stories about money trouble would help you if you had the same kind of trouble."—"I like to listen to other people's troubles. It is like finding out what goes on in the world."

It is true that problems solved by fictional characters may serve as models for real-life solutions. Thus, if the story shows how a delicate marital situation can be handled satisfactorily, the listener may be encouraged to attempt a similar solution, which he might otherwise have considered too difficult. In certain cases, however, this kind of escape into low levels of reality may leave with some listeners the feeling that to solve a problem they need only indulge in pious declarations and wishful thinking, or to escape into a dream-world like that of daytime serials and other forms of popular literature. Furthermore, fictional solutions of problems cannot compensate for the listener's feelings of inadequacy. No matter how hard he tries to relieve his feeling of inferiority by listening to heroic exploits, or to identify himself with the hero, his original feeling of inferiority will persist.

Listeners reported several reasons why they prefer radio dramas to other forms of literature. It seems that our educational system, which too often forces "good literature" upon us at a time when we are not psychologically ready for it, has made many of us consider any kind of serious literature as if it were an assignment, an unpleasant task. People have developed a sort of inferiority feeling about good literature. They regard it as too complicated for them, or too time-consuming. They welcome daytime serials or other types of diversion that might provide the same kind of satisfaction, but in a simpler and more palatable form. It is therefore futile to debate the question whether or not daytime serials should be continued. If they were not made available, something very similar to them would undoubtedly be developed, if not through the radio, then through other media of communication.

We may better appreciate the influence of radio dramas as forms of literature if we consider the historical origin of drama and of fiction. Whenever primitive people were in trouble, they invented games and ceremonials wherein their problems were dramatized in such a way that the solutions were integrated into the stories. The idea of these primitive folk was to influence the gods by showing them how the people wanted their problems to be solved. It was like saying to the superhuman forces of the universe, "This is how I want you to arrange my destiny." Even in modern times, peasants in the Balkans who want more rain suggest their idea to God through rituals and religious ceremonies. Perhaps the happy endings of most fiction can be traced to such efforts of primitive man to influence the gods in behalf of human needs and goals. Radio dramas today, while not based on prayer or religious mysticism, perform a similar psychological function. They make life easier. We might add that they would do so more effectively if they were better integrated with other forms of mass communication, such as newspapers, periodicals, and books. All these instruments for the sharing of knowledge should be improved and co-ordinated in order to advance the goals of democratic living.

Radio has tremendous educational potentialities. It combines many characteristics of drama, concert, theater, forum, newspaper, and church. It can provide the best in entertainment and instruction for every corner of the land and for all who can afford to buy an inexpensive receiver. With the further development of FM and television, many cultural advantages of the nation can be made available to all.

# PART III

## WINNING SOCIAL PRESTIGE

None of us lives alone. Even in the privacy of our homes or in the most secluded spot we can find, we live with the ideas and personalities of other people. Also, we live with ourselves in the sense that we are able to discover and appreciate our own qualities of personality. We want others to respect us and we want to respect ourselves. In this way we derive a sense of power and we satisfy our deep yearning to influence the course of events. What are the psychological factors which govern this basic desire for winning social prestige and self-respect? Our nation-wide surveys provide significant information as to how we seek "social satisfactions" from the use of everyday products such as soap, clothes, and cosmetics.

In our democratic society the aim is to help each individual to become worthy of social acceptance and recognition. This aim can be achieved only if we provide opportunities for all our people to become efficient in everyday living. Men must understand each other and themselves if they are to work together toward the goals of a democracy. And the psychologist can contribute much to mutual understanding by disclosing the psychological forces which influence our people as consumers and as citizens. The kind of products he buys and the way he uses them reveal a great deal about the psychological motives and needs of the individual.

The old folks at home listen to a sentimental episode.

According to the advertisers, the number of friends we make, the amount of romance and adventure in our lives, the success of our marriage and of our business, all depend on soap. Irrespective of this, about 4,000,000,000 pounds of soap are sold annually in the United States alone, and this cake of soap, this insignificant bit of lye and potash, seems to be a most valuable piece of property.

American advertisers are spending about $32,000,000 a year to convince the average citizen that the yearned for love and romance will come to him if he will only agree to use certain brands of soap.

Not only magazine and newspaper columns but also radio programs are used to propagandize the miraculous effects of soap. More than twelve per cent of the income of the major radio networks is derived from sponsors of daytime serials. Because of their sponsorship, the stories are popularly known as "soap operas." In these stories nobody uses soap in any ostentatious way, but the characters experience friendship and romance, marriage and love, in some form or another. By association with the program, the soaps advertised take on a similar romantic aura.

} 113 {

The Lux Radio Theatre, which is said to attract the largest audience of any single show, uses the intermissions to interview famous moving picture stars, who stress the fact that they acquired their beauty primarily by using Lux toilet soap.

The psychologist is not interested in the truth or falsehood of such claims. He *is* interested in the fact that a simple everyday commodity like soap has been advertised as a means of satisfying the important human need for beauty and happiness. He looks at the American scene in the same way as an anthropologist would study the behavior of an African tribe. If we assume this scientific attitude, we shall be amazed to discover how significant is each of our everyday habits. Why, then, does so much glamor surround a mere piece of soap, which, after all, has no function except to dissolve grime and thus help to wash dirt off our faces and bodies?

Nor has the romantic appeal of soap been restricted to women. Men, too, though not concerned so much with glamor, are reminded that they can attract the opposite sex only if they avoid body odors. In fact, for years extensive advertising campaigns have tried to convince the male of the species that he suffers from body odor, and that this is why most girls reject him.

In this way, soap is connected with the fundamental needs and desires of human beings. It is only one example of the main point of this discussion: that our everyday habits have a much deeper basis than we ordinarily assume. An apparently meaningless habit which we pursue day after day may express some vital submerged impulse that we thought we had suppressed or overcome. *If we really understand why people behave as they do—we shall be more tolerant of the apparently senseless peculiarities of other people.* Happiness depends as much on these little things of everyday living as on the broad ideals of liberty, democracy, fraternity.

Like our desires and habits, the commodities we use can be traced back to primitive times. Soap has a very long history; and bathing, so closely connected with it, is even more ancient. The Teutons and the Celts are reported to have made a product of this kind. A number of well-equipped soap factories have been unearthed in the excavations at Pompeii. Commercial soap is said to have been manufactured in Marseilles as early as the thirteenth century. On the coast of the Mediterranean were located most of the soap makers of Europe, in the great trade centers of Venice, Milan, and Florence. These places were near the sources of olive oil, which was then an essential ingredient of soap.

In early America, soap making, like many other trades, was a home industry requiring a high degree of skill. The modern housewife who saved the fat dripping from her pans, to help in the war effort, was doing just about what the pioneer woman or the settler had to do when preparing to make soap. It is reported that soap manufacturing as a business was started in Jamestown, by German and Polish immigrants skilled in the art, but these enterprises remained small until, in 1806, Will Colgate built a soap factory for large-scale production. Since then the industry has steadily expanded until now its total annual business amounts to more than $300,000,000.

The long history of soap can be explained only by the fact that the product must have satisfied the vital needs of people, and must have appealed to human desires that have persisted throughout the ages. Today people use soap for the very same reasons as in the Middle Ages in Europe, or in the Colonial Period in America. Let us inquire into these reasons. Now, let us see.

## Why We Use Soap

Why do we use soap? To get clean, you will say. But we could get clean in other ways. Therefore we must look further for an explanation. Actually, we use soap because it is *pleasant to touch.*

Soap is one of the few products in direct contact with our bodies. Recently, we handed a few cakes of soap to a group of people and watched their reactions. What do you suppose is one of the first things most of them did? No, they did not look at the soap especially or begin to talk about it. They merely slid their fingers over its surface; they wanted to see how the soap would feel when it touched the skin.

Soap is smooth, very smooth when it is wet, and we all like this feeling of smoothness. We like to touch glass. Children love to press their noses against smooth mirrors or window panes. We enjoy touching baby's skin—it is so nice and smooth. For the same reason, pipe smokers enjoy caressing the smooth bowl of a favorite pipe. After men shave, they are delighted with the smoothness of the skin, and take great pains to get rid of the slightest spot of roughness.

Why does smoothness make such a strong appeal to us? It is because our hands are like a sensitive machine which connects us with the world of things, giving us pleasure or pain or other feelings. If we close our eyes and touch an object, we are very sure it is before us. Touching it proves its qualities of hardness, smoothness, weight, dryness, or wetness. The desire to touch things is so powerful that museums all over the world have to post signs to keep people from touching valuable exhibits. When we touch an object or a person, we feel closer to the thing we touch; this degree of intimacy is absent if we merely look without touching.

Touching soap or any other smooth surface is pleasant, and the skin in all parts of the body can give us pleasure

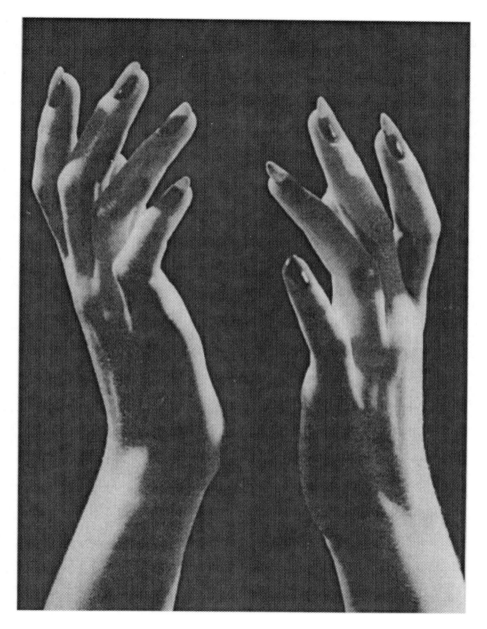

Our hands are like a sensitive machine.

through the sense of touch. The palms of our hands can give us intense pleasure, probably for the biological reason that the human race had to reach for things and get a good grip on them in order to survive and develop. Our ancestors passed on to us these everyday habits of touching, handling, and gripping objects. So now, one of the first activities of a new-born baby is to clasp an object in his palm. An adult acts the same way when he clutches soap firmly in his hand.

Another point about soap is its weight. As one of the people whom we interviewed said: "When soap is heavy, you know that you're getting your money's worth . . . that it's not just full of air."

Do we really care about "getting our money's worth"? Most of us have a peculiar feeling of guilt if we let a cake of soap melt in water. "I wouldn't pick up a dime, but I feel sinful if I leave soap in water," one of our soap users admitted. "I would hardly bend down to pick up a nickel," said another, "but I feel bad when I see soap lying in water." This is typical of the attitude of many people toward economizing on soap.

Like soap, bread is a mass product of very little money value in this country, and yet few people can throw out bread or waste it in any other way, without feeling sinful and wicked. This attitude is probably a relic of the early days when making soap and bread was a costly or tedious affair.

Most of us prefer soap that is heavy. Objects that are heavy impress us as being more solid or reliable than those that are light. And this respect for weight has carried over into our everyday language. We refer to a "weighty" cause or argument, and we say, "He threw the weight of his personality into the balance," or, in the popular phrase, "He likes to throw his weight around."

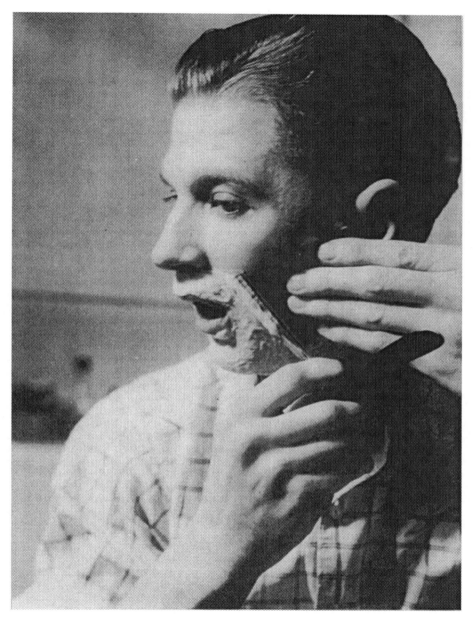

At great pains to get rid of the slightest spot of roughness.

Even the shape of soap affects our preference for a particular kind or brand. A housewife said: "I like a soap you can get a good grip on . . . It's like everything in life. . . . . You like to get a good grip on things." Most people like a soap with a rounded, broad surface that fits into the palm of the hand and enables them to "get a good grip on it." This idea has also affected our ways of speaking. We say, "He grasps the situation," "Get hold of yourself," and "The matter is beyond his grasp." We don't like a cake of soap which is too thin or which has sharp edges, because we cannot hold it tight in the palm and we therefore feel dissatisfied or frustrated.

Soap odor is, of course, significant in the purchase of this commodity, as indicated by such comments as: "I don't like that soap. . . . I just can't imagine myself smelling like that."—"It's so much pleasure to sit in the tub and have the soap perfume permeate my whole being."—"I hate body odors," confided a thirty-seven-year-old woman, "and always have a fear of having them. I am much more fussy about the cleanliness of my body than about the cleanliness of my house. I would not give any part of my body a chance to let me know that it could offend."

But not all people dislike such odors. Sometimes, those who protest most strongly possess an inhibited strong desire to smell certain odors. Some of them love their own perspiration and really enjoy being dirty. "I consciously look for the odor of perspiration," said one of these individuals. "When I'm playing golf, I may be hot and sweaty but that is not offensive to me, because that is the order of things."

Next to their favorite soap, many people prefer soap that is white. White is associated with purity. They suspect that coloring is used to conceal impurities in the soap. Such people will accept a colored brand only if the color is justified by advertising which, for example, extols the value of palm and olive oils. When we asked a group to select their preferred soap from among thirty-five well-known brands, they invariably chose the soap they were using regularly at the time, but their second choice was the soap with the greatest degree of whiteness, the most highly finished and glossy surface, the sharpest contour, and the most marked appearance of newness. They liked new cakes. As one person said, "I get an added feeling of luxury when I take a bath with a new cake of soap." Some of them admitted that they sometimes washed off a used cake, but preferred a new one, or at least a soap which no one else had used. In this way they avoided breaking the personal contact and psychological relationship between the cake of soap and their own bodies.

You may have noticed that many people like to pick out their soap from a large supply on the grocer's shelves. Mass display induces them to buy even when they do not need the product. This can be explained by the fact that they may have run short of soap in the past, and have a vague memory of that unpleasant experience. At any rate, they hoard soap. One of the hoarders told us this illuminating story:

"I have a peculiar habit with soap. It is something which has followed me ever since my early childhood—a strange whim that I still indulge in when traveling. As you know, in the good hotels one always receives nice little cakes of soap every morning. There's a small cake for the hands and a slightly larger one for the bath. I hoard these. The maid may leave two or three each morning. Two of them I hide in the drawer, until it takes a good part of the suitcase to accommodate these cakes of soap. One place I did this and the maid facetiously remarked I must like to keep clean because I was using so much soap. However, she must have found my supply and kept replenishing me from that, unknown to me.

I discovered, later, what she had done, for, after a week in one hotel out West, I thought, having nothing to do just then, I'd count my little hoard of soap. To my utter astonishment, I had only the same amount I had had the week before, and still I had been replenishing the supply by as much as three cakes a day."

*Washing and Bathing*

Most of us are accustomed to taking a bath several times a week. Bathing is, on first thought, a simple matter of getting clean. But when we let people tell us in their own words how they feel when taking a bath, they have a lot to say about this prosaic habit. Here, for instance, are some typical remarks: "When I am in the tub, Doris Cromwell has nothing on me. . . ."—"I always sing in the tub; for those few minutes I don't have to buy a steak, or scrub the floor, or mind the children."

Few of the people we talked to, however, mentioned the romance and beauty stressed by modern advertisements. Instead, they used such very human words as those mentioned above. These expressions tell us much more about the real fun and pleasure derived from bathing than the fancy terms, like "facial cocktails" and "beauty lather," used by copywriters. But how is it possible, in this cynical world of ours, for so much significance to be attached to bathing? Only a psychological analysis can give us the answer.

While washing and bathing, we are alone and our minds are free to roam. We can use the time to make plans, to take stock of ourselves, to examine our bodies in the strong light over the bathroom mirror, or just to daydream.

Bathing time is a pleasant interlude during which we are not constrained to think and work hard. Many of us look forward to this period of relaxation. We have the feeling that we can "wash our troubles away." Bathing takes on a special psychological function because it coincides with the beginning or ending of a day, or even a week. It provides the deep gratification of figuratively getting rid of the past and being able to start again with renewed hope—getting a new start. The bath implies finishing a task, reminiscing about the day's work, and preparing to begin the new day with fresh vigor.

This desire for renewal is so strong that people like to have their sheets, linen, and everything else crisp and new. "I don't enjoy a bath unless I can have everything 100 per cent new and clean."

People shed their adult dignity in the bathroom. One woman confessed: "I feel like a kid again when I am in the tub." Another dignified matron said: "I lie on my stomach and play like a child. I blow bubbles and I drape my knees over the side of the tub and I sing. I have a wonderful time and like to move up and down and make waves."

In our interviews with children we discovered that they use soap as a toy, and that bathing stimulates ingenious play. They let the soap slide down the tub in "chute-the-chutes" fashion, and they propel it around the tub by moving the water with their hands. They duck under the water, play dead, or imagine themselves to be submarines.

Adults, too, play in the bathtub, and the feeling of being a child again is quite common. A man or a woman takes off dignity with clothes. Splashing the water, popping the soap from between the hands, whistling or singing without restraint—these are familiar adult experiences.

When we are in the bathtub, we give full play to our imagination. "Sometimes I am a maharajah when I am in the tub," said one. The bathroom becomes a dream world. Inside the bathtub is a world totally different from that out-

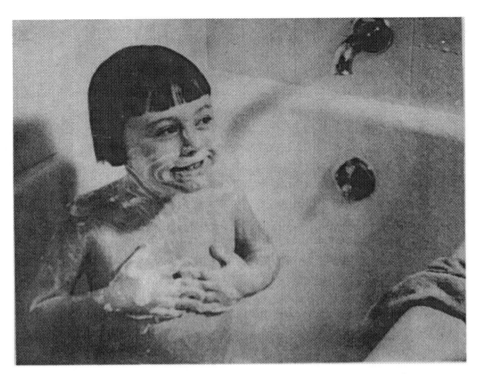

Ewing Galloway

Bathing stimulates ingenious play.

side. Everything connected with bathing—the feeling of iso-
lation, the freedom from clothes, the distinctive qualities
of water, the release from reality—all these work in one direction, to give free rein to the imagination. "I can be anyone
I please in the tub," is a remark typical of this attitude. And
this freedom is closely tied up with the feeling of luxury. As
one of our respondents stated: "Soap provides luxury for a
dime. Even people who are not wealthy have to get a feeling
of luxury once in a while, even if it's only from a cake of
soap."

Statements like these, taken from our case histories, show
clearly that people enjoy a feeling of luxury and absorb some
of the glamor attached to knowing that they can use the
same soap as the moving picture stars and the débutantes.

Bathing and washing seem also to have an effect of moral purification. Thus, Pilate washed his hands, indicating that he did not want to be held responsible for the crucifixion of Jesus. Baptism is a sort of washing, and, in certain religions, the priests must wash themselves completely before starting the ritual service. Nor has the symbolic significance of washing and bathing been entirely lost in our modern times. One of our respondents reported that after taking a bath she "feels like an angel." After bathing, people feel cleaner in a moral as well as a physical sense.

Washing and bathing give us a feeling of accomplishment, expressed in remarks such as, "I like to watch the dirt roll off." The primitive wish to be dirty is deep-rooted. A child has to be taught a long time before he can distinguish between being clean and being dirty. Interest in cleanliness and in hygiene is relatively new in the story of civilization. Psychologically, every bath is a victory for civilized man over his subconscious wish to be dirty. For this reason, we cannot help feeling a real sense of achievement whenever we bathe. We have "done our duty." And we get more "kick" out of washing our hands when they are unusually dirty; the dirtier the water, the cleaner we feel.

Bathing gives us the pleasant sensation of release from gravity. "I feel twenty pounds lighter," said one of the women we interviewed. When we step into the tub and lie down, the water seems to "take a heavy load away" from us. We feel lighter, and we actually are lighter. Floating provides definite pleasure. Although we cannot float in the bathtub, we can let our arms and legs float. The desire to use a full tub of water, to be completely covered by water, is a wish frequently expressed by those whom we interviewed, and it is connected with our desire to cheat gravity. We discovered, further, that individuals who are physically handicapped—

paralytics, fat people, old people—find in bathing a kind of ego restoration. The water buoys up their limbs so that their movements are no longer hampered.

In the bathroom, we have an opportunity to inspect our bodies. Said one elderly gentleman: "I check myself over." We compare ourselves with our ideal, decide whether we are too fat or too thin, discover pimples and skin blemishes. From our interviews we found, also, that often one of the first actions after stepping out of the tub is to wipe the mirror in order to inspect one's body.

*Lather Works Like Magic*

People have a vague idea that something miraculous takes place under the cover of lather, which seems to work like a magic veil. They expect a kind of wonderful transformation. They want rich lather from the soap they buy. As one gentleman expressed this expectation, "I want a lot of show for my money." They derive intense satisfaction out of working up lather while bathing. They feel that they are really creating something, satisfying this impelling urge to handle, shape, and build objects. They may even use the lather on their faces or bodies to form strange shapes, in a sort of masquerading.

Bubble baths and the glamor attached to them reflect the deep gratification provided by lather. The lightness and "unreal" character of lather "born out of foam" has much significance. Lather has a caressing effect on the skin, which explains why people soap themselves more than would be necessary if they merely wanted to get clean. The urge to caress ourselves is a deep-seated, complicated psychological tendency which we usually try to suppress. Soap and lather supply an accepted pretext to fulfill this natural desire to pat and smooth our skin.

Lather has a caressing effect on the skin.

In one sense, our skin is our *ego façade*. Skin reflects the whole personality. Our first impressions of others depend largely on the appearance of their skin. When the advertiser promises to help us develop a smooth and "lovely" skin, he is using a most potent appeal. Skin also reflects the condition of our health, the environment in which we live—even our state of mind. When we are embarrassed we blush; when we are afraid we blanch; when we are enraged, we grow purple; when we are sick, we turn pale.

*Suggestions*

There is a practical value in understanding these psychological facts about bathing. They help to rid us of superstitions, fears, and inhibitions. Perhaps you like to soap yourself twice because you enjoy touching your body. There is nothing wrong with such a desire; it's a natural one. So there is no need to feel sinful or wicked about it. One young lady reported that she soaped her entire body heavily with lather and then let the shower remove the lather gradually. To the psychologist there is nothing immoral about the idea that she is actually allowing the shower to undress her. He understands that this girl is merely enjoying the psychological feeling of magic connected with lather. She is being mentally reborn under the lather, and she expectantly waits for the shower to reveal a miraculous transformation in her appearance.

When buying products such as soap, consider the real qualities of the products, not the romantic advertisements or the glamorous radio programs. Note that such appeals have nothing to do with intrinsic values. Note, also, that most people are swayed by forces of which they are entirely unaware. They may buy a product because they wish to be admired, for instance, or because they feel lonely and insecure, and they feel convinced that the product will help them obtain admiration or a sense of security, as the case may be. Try to find the reasons why people behave as they do, and you will become more tolerant of their peculiarities.

There is really nothing wrong about pinning your hope of beauty and success on a bit of tallow and potash. If you look for promised miracles, you will probably be disappointed, but if you think of body care and cleanliness as important aspects of self-appreciation and security, some of your fond expectations may be fulfilled. Even a simple cake of soap may offer you unexpected satisfaction if you think of it not as a sober or boring necessity but rather as an opportunity for self-expression. Be a "grown-up" child and get a thrill out of the little things of everyday living.

# Chuse thy clothes by thine own eyes, not another's !

Why do most people get excited about new fashions in clothes? And why especially in spring?

Human beings are not alone in this affectation. Many other animals are interested in outward appearance. Birds do not have clothing stores. They grow their own new feathers instead of pasting or sewing them on. And it would be a poor sparrow indeed who did not renew his plumage at least once a year. Among human beings, women are influenced more than men by the desire for self-display. Among other animals, however, it is usually the male who does his "remodeling and repainting" when spring comes along. In both cases, the purpose is to attract the opposite sex. Most animals make no attempt to conceal this purpose, but human beings are not so frank about biological functions. Even older women who do not go out of their way to attract men are as thrilled as a débutante about the new spring clothes.

With most animals, the male takes the initiative in wooing, and this is why it is the male who makes use of self-decoration. With human beings, as men may suspect but hesitate to admit, the female takes the initiative in attracting the opposite sex. And sometimes, feminine aggression starts at an early age. Here are some illuminating remarks by one of the "weaker" sex:

"Thirteen years old — oh, yes — that was a turning point. Up to that time I had minor crushes on boys in my class. Then, when I was thirteen, I met a boy and I became very much infatuated with him. I remember at that time I had gotten a green leather jacket and a green skirt. Not a loose-fitting skirt, it was a very nice tight-fitting one. The jacket was very right, too. I felt very attractive in it. It gave me a feeling of power and confidence. "

The primitive sexual basis for self-display has been modified considerably as human beings have climbed to the uppermost rungs of the ladder of evolution. Man has developed interest in decoration *per se*. Now our appreciation of beauty develops early in life. Very young children, even one-year-olds, enjoy wearing a scrap of paper or a ribbon in their hair. Apes, who are in many ways like children or primitive people, take delight in ornamentation. The psychologist Wolfgang Koehler, who has made extensive studies of apes, reports: "Almost daily the animals can be seen walking about with a rope, a bit of rag, a blade of grass, or a twig on their shoulders. . . . Their pleasure is visibly increased by draping things round themselves. No observer can escape the impression that . . . the objects hanging about the body serve the purpose of adornment in the widest sense."

We decorate ourselves, nowadays, not only to attract the other sex, but also to become outstanding, conspicuous. A child, proudly showing everybody her new dress, knows that the dress is an effective means of gaining admiration, interest, and love. We all want to be superior, to possess characteristics which are unmistakably our own. As one of our own respondents said: "Now when I go to buy clothes, I look for certain things. I know what to took for. I know what suits my taste and personality." We like to be more attractive than others, more alert, and better dressed, but we do not want to be too conspicuous, as that would tend to isolate us from our social group.

## Fashion Is "Ambivalent"

Clothes fulfill a twofold or, as the psychologists say, an "ambivalent" purpose. They help us to be different from others, but still enough like them to be accepted in our circle of acquaintances. Fashion and our interest in spring clothes reflect this ambivalence. We want a new hat, different from the old one. We dislike the one we have been wearing. We want a hat that represents an individual design, an original idea. Nor do we want the same style of hat worn by our neighbor. If we see anyone wearing a hat like our own, our feelings are mixed. We say, "There goes my hat," and we are pleased because the wearer agrees with our "good taste" —but we are also somewhat disturbed, much as we feel disturbed when someone uses our cake of soap or eats from our plate.

If we buy a hat so unusual that people turn to stare at it, we lack the courage to wear it—until we see another person with the same kind of hat. Then we experience a feeling of relief. This desire to follow the fashion has social significance. People whose dress is up-to-date belong to a social group different from that of people who wear old-fashioned apparel. On that basis of distinction, sometimes the price of a new hat is enough to make us feel that we are acceptable members of an up-to-date social group.

Often the clothes we wear serve as outward symbols of our occupations or of our social status. In ancient times, the "symbolism" in this respect was far more marked. Nobles and patricians wore garments which were actually forbid-

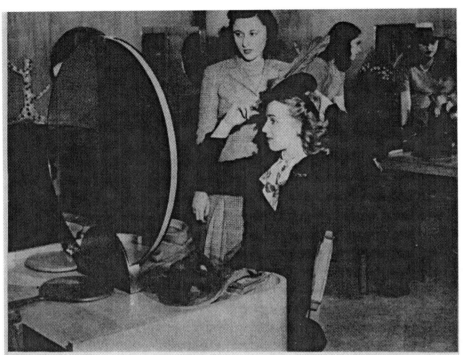

She wants a new hat, different from the old one.

den to the lower classes. The Nazis of modern Germany forced the Jews to wear a yellow star as evidence of membership in a persecuted group, and this made it easy for the Nazis to oppress the Jews. In our own society, it is illegal for a civilian to wear a military uniform. Because of their clothes, we tend to contrast the city slicker with the home-loving farmer; the sloppy Frenchman with the neat and sporty Englishman; the nonchalant American with the stiff and precise German. Clothes become symbolic expressions of caste and national character.

### Furs and Trophies

A mink coat is a sign of social prestige, primarily because it is expensive. Only those who are "extremely well off" can afford it. Thus, it is one indication of success, as the world gauges success. This psychological and social distinction can be traced back to primitive ages. The hunter who had killed a dangerous beast wore decorative clothes or trophies to impress others with his prowess. Nowadays, thousands of years afterward, our elegant ladies, who do not hunt their victims in jungle or forest, still wear certain kinds of clothes as trophies, proclaiming to the world their superiority or wealth.

Most psychologists agree that clothes have a threefold purpose: decoration, modesty, and protection. All three purposes are interrelated. Even a fig leaf to hide our nakedness has a decorative effect. An expensive fur coat which protects us from the cold is also a trophy, a symbol of financial success and power. The fig leaf in the Garden of Eden hid the shame of the first human beings, served them as a form of decoration and, in a moral and physical sense, helped to protect the delicate sex organs.

### "The Apparel Oft Proclaims the Man"

For thousands of years human beings have worn clothes. Most of us wear some kind of apparel from infancy to death. So it is not surprising that our clothes are very closely related to our personality. Often they reflect our character as individuals. "For the apparel oft proclaims the man," wrote Shakespeare. "To step into somebody else's shoes" is a significant remark. It implies assuming the actual personality of that other person.

Most of us develop a psychological attachment to our wearing apparel. One woman described her feelings about one of her dresses as follows: "I can still conjure up the way this dress felt on my body. I loved the touch of it and, also the smell of it. It had a peculiar smell all its own. It was the first tailored suit I ever had. I can still see the pattern of the design on it. It had large squares, and was gray. It had also a little bit of the atmosphere of the city I lived in that time, the people I knew then, and the things that happened. I remember lying in the grass with it on. It was nothing glamorous. I felt at home in it. It belonged to me in a deeper sense of the word."

Clothes are an extension of ourselves. A run in a stocking or a torn seam can destroy our self-assurance. Knowledge that we are well dressed can give us a comfortable feeling of security. It has been said: "The consciousness of being well dressed may bestow a peace such as religion cannot give."

## The Body Image

We all have a body image of ourselves, a definite idea of our outward appearance and inner character. Our clothes should not conceal, but should rather express, and accentuate our personality. One of our respondents put it this way: "I'm extremely fond of the dress. It is not revealing in a sensuous sense, but very feminine and flattering. It's tight-fitting, clings halfway up the hip line; the neck is low but not to where it reveals the bosom. I remember when I went to get it. I went to a wholesale house. I thought the dress practical and beautiful. It is navy blue. My mother didn't want me to get it. She didn't feel it was attractive enough. Sometimes a person feels, with a certain piece of clothes, that it just expresses one and is a part of one. I felt that way about this dress."

A woman who overdresses or wears clothes suitable for a younger person, but not for her, is usually trying to hide her true self. Such a person is afraid to accept herself as she really is. But, once she decides that her real self is nothing to be ashamed of, she will dress in a more appropriate manner that will improve her appearance. She will wear clothes that fit her in a psychological, as well as in a physical, sense. A person with good taste in clothes first of all has an accurate image of herself, and then selects apparel which fits that image.

Sometimes, however, instead of merely fitting into our mood, clothes actually modify our behavior and personality. Thus, a child with a white dress or a new suit becomes temporarily more demure or placid. When adults put on sports clothes, they gain psychological, as well as physical, freedom. A woman dressed in an evening gown tends to walk more slowly than usual and to act in a more "ladylike" manner. The following comment reflects this influence of clothes on personality: "I just remember everyone used to tell me that I looked well in blue. First I accepted everyone's opinion, but I felt blue to be a weak color. I felt weak in it, not daring and dashing as in green. Green is my favorite color. I always felt sentimental about green. Nature itself is green. Anything green excites me. I like it very much. I also remember certain novels I read, and whenever the author described a daring dashing heroine, she would wear 'siphon,' and when she wore green she was particularly daring and strong and would dare to defy society. I suppose that appealed to me."

*A Feeling of Security*

The degree of freedom allowed by our clothes may provide a clue to our personality. A man who consistently chooses clothes that look stiff and formal may be suffering from a feeling of insecurity. Perhaps he wears a hard outer shell to cover a weaker inside kernel. The chances are that a person who wears no hat, and who prefers informal clothes, is more willing to show his inner self to others. These generalizations do not, of course, apply to all cases, but merely indicate that clothes both reflect and affect personality. That is why some individuals wear apparel that is quite at variance with the prevailing fashion.

## Imitation

In choosing our clothes we sometimes tend to imitate people whom we admire, scarcely realizing that we are imitating them. Moving pictures have had a great influence on clothing styles. We identify ourselves with a hero or a heroine whose taste in clothes sways our own preferences. The judgment of people with whom we associate, especially relatives whom we respect, modifies our decisions. Frequently, children like to wear the type of clothes worn by their parents, although sometimes a child will insist on choosing styles radically different from those of the parents. In either case, the development of the individual's taste in clothes is influenced by early association with people who are accepted as ideals. Herein is a clue to what he would like to be, to his character, and thus there may be some justification for our tendency to judge people by their clothes. Our judgment is affected by their choice of style, not by the quality or the cost. An overdressed person not only shows poor taste, but also reveals a frustrated personality. Such people try to use these psychological crutches to hold themselves up to the attention and affection of others.

## Shoes and Inferiority

People behave in a peculiar way when buying shoes. Our researches disclose that many people feel embarrassed when they take their shoes off. The shoe salesman is aware of this feeling. He knows that, once he has induced the customer to take off her shoes, he is pretty sure to make the sale. Perhaps the feeling of embarrassment or of inferiority is caused by fear of having a hole in the stocking. It may also have a deeper significance. When we take off our shoes, we are, in a sense, undressing in the presence of a stranger. Then, too, in ancient times, walking barefoot or in stockings was a symbol of servitude and humiliation. It may be that this slight feeling of inferiority has persisted throughout the ages and still affects us when we are being fitted for shoes.

Furthermore, we lose height when we take off our shoes— and losing height connotes losing prestige. Recently the use of special shoes to make short people appear taller has been emphasized in advertisements directed to men who are "shorter than she is."

New shoes have a decided effect on our behavior. If we watch people carefully as they leave a shoe store, we notice

The right kind of hat gives us dignity.

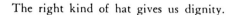

*Ewing Galloway*

that they put their feet down in a hesitant and self-conscious way. They like to listen to the squeaking that many new shoes produce. For a while, too, they may get a shine more frequently than they ordinarily would.

### Look at Your Hat

The right kind of hat give us dignity and real individuality. This is particularly true of men's hats. Women's hats are dictators; they impose iron rules. There is only one way they can be put on, irrespective of the wearer's mood. She may be in heaven—but even if her heart is broken and her spirits are in the depths, the feather in her hat will be pointed toward the sky. A lady's hat is not permitted to reflect her emotions.

How different are men's hats! When a man buys a new one, it may look like all the others. But as soon as he takes it into his warm and understanding hands, it seems to come alive. His personality is mirrored in the way he shapes his hat. A strange, impersonal hat becomes, after a few days, Mr. Brown's hat and his only. Nobody else creases a hat exactly as he does.

Several problems related to the psychology of hats remain unsolved. Why don't women take off their hats when greeting someone, and why don't men take off their coats or other wearing apparel instead of their hats? As a matter of fact, in the Middle East and in parts of Asia, people remove their shoes to show respect. Imagine what would happen if, on our crowded streets, a gentleman had to sit down and take off his shoes whenever he greeted a lady! Our men have an easy time of it. Most of us accept the traditional forms of greeting. Beau Brummel, however, refused to take off his hat: "He never took off his hat to anyone, not even to a lady; it would have been difficult to replace it in the same position, for it was invariably put on with great care and at a prescribed angle; added to which, his wig might have been disturbed—a catastrophe too dreadful to be wantonly encountered." *

After all, psychologically a hat is merely a portable roof. Raising the hat opens a door to the individual's privacy. He says in effect, "Look here. I have no secrets. I invite you to be my friend." More than being an act of greeting, raising the hat reflects our mood. Men tear off their hats during an exciting moment at a football game. When we feel depressed, we may pull our hat down over our ears. Such action reflects our tendency to draw away from others, and serves as a protective device; or it may be a sign of aggression and defiance, in which case we may pull our hat down to our eyes. How fierce we can then look at an adversary! We can watch him out of a corner of our eye, but he cannot see our expression. In the same way as eyes and eyelids, a hat can give us an aggressive appearance. For instance, suppose we turn the head to one side and then look straight ahead, with head lowered and eyelids partly closed. This gives us an appearance of extreme defiance and aggressiveness, especially if we shake a fist or gnash the teeth. Every bit of this pantomime has biological significance. Primitive men tried to conceal the expression in their eyes so that an enemy could not anticipate their next move, and they protected part of their faces from a possible surprise assault. They gnashed their teeth to warn the enemy that they meant to tear him apart. Even in our modern culture, these primitive reactions are imitated in our use of a hat to show aggression. As Oliver Wendell Holmes has said: "The hat is the *ultimum moriens* —the last dying spark of respectability."

* Lewis Melville, *Beau Brummel, His Life & Letters*—1924.

*Clothes for Better Living*

The costumes of a people may reveal a great deal about their philosophy and ways of living. Men have often fought for the right to wear a costume honored by tradition and national pride. When the Nazis compelled Germans to wear brown shirts, they were not merely starting a fad—they were making such clothes a symbol of power and unity. Douglas Jerrold was not altogether wrong when he said: "Be sure of it, everything in life depends upon the cock of the hat."

Many of our clothes preferences, however, are irrational. Deep-seated psychological factors that are not always logical lead us to accept or reject a specific type of garment. This is why we keep wearing unnecessary things, instead of devising new and more practical kinds of clothing. The process of changing such habits is a slow one, for social customs involve numerous long-established attitudes, preferences, and traditions. Perhaps some day, after we have learned to control our emotions and to behave in a truly reasonable way, we shall plan our clothes so that they will combine the utmost of freedom and individuality with adequate provision for the three main purposes of apparel: decoration, modesty, and protection.

*Suggestions*

Understanding the real causes of your clothing preferences may help you to adapt them to your true personality. Perhaps you have been influenced more by inhibitions, feelings of insecurity, and emotional impulses than by intelligent reasoning. Perhaps you need more courage and understanding so that you will dare to dress in a more informal and comfortable costume; or perhaps you are wearing ill-fitting informal clothes as compensation for lack of self-confidence.

Choose clothes that express your personality, but do not

stray too far from the fashion in your community. Avoid the temptation to imitate slavishly the dress of others. Dress in accordance with your age. Do not use clothes as psychological crutches to gain the attention and affection of others. Remember that a person of good taste understands his or her own personality and chooses clothes that fit the personality.

# irror, Mirror...

(COSMETICS)

What we see in our mirror has a tremendous influence on our everyday behavior. Looking in the mirror is the only way to meet ourselves, literally, face to face: "When you look well, you feel well and want to be seen."

Each of us has a mental picture of himself. But our mirror confronts us with reality, which does not often conform with that mental picture. In the privacy of our homes, we can discover blemishes or deficiencies. This does not discourage us so much as adverse criticism by other people. Still, a person who is oversensitive may dislike to look into a mirror. He does not want to be reminded of the facts. As one young lady put it: "I had a magnifying mirror, but whenever I looked into it, it drove me crazy. So I finally threw it away."

Although women use cosmetics primarily to be admired by others, make-up involves certain other psychological factors. In many cases the use of cosmetics has become a vital need, irrespective of social prestige, as witness these comments by a lady who was unusually frank: "I make up for myself. Even if I were alone at home I would make up. Even if I were existing alone in the world I'd make up." Another . one said: "I always use make-up when I'm home alone. I think it raises your morale. You feel more attractive and

Cosmetics provide psychological therapy.

well groomed." Such remarks prove that cosmetics profoundly affect the individual's everyday living.

## Cosmetics for Self-Improvement

For one thing, cosmetics help the user to get rid of an awareness of personal inferiority, real or imagined. The woman whose features are imperfect, as compared with her ideal, applies cosmetics to improve her appearance. This helps her to compensate for imperfections and to get rid of feelings of inferiority. Cosmetics thus provide a form of psychological therapy, as attested by statements such as these: "I like to make up. It's pleasant to improve anything by your own efforts, even your face." "It's a constant source of amazement to me how I improve when I put make-up on." Because we look better, we feel better. The use of cosmetics helps us to improve ourselves, to reach toward an ideal image, to enhance our ego.

From infancy on, we gradually develop an awareness of our need of self-improvement. At first, an infant's sole interest, love, and desires—his libido—are centered in himself. But soon he becomes aware that other people are affected by his behavior. Their reactions cause him to compare himself with others, and he then sees that he does not measure up to his ideal. The rest of his lifetime, he may be striving to get rid of some feeling of inferiority in order that he may be able to return, once again, to the infant's perfect satisfaction with himself. Cosmetics are supposed to ease the way toward this goal of self-satisfaction.

Progress toward a stage of self-sufficiency, however, is slow and gradual. Advertisers of cosmetics who know their business do not depend mainly on beautiful pictures to influence their public. In fact, if the lady in an advertisement is too beautiful, she may discourage many girls. They will realize that they can never hope to reach such an ideal within any reasonable time. Such advertisements may even antagonize people for the very reason that they seem to hold up an unattainable ideal. Therefore, the heroine must be pretty but not too far from familiar reality, so that the reader can at least hope to achieve a similar complexion or esthetic effect. The skillful advertiser helps people to build their own *attain-*

*able* ideal or wishful self-portrait, and then he presents, step by step, the positive aid which his product can provide. He does not say, "You did not brush your teeth, so look what happened." Instead he says, "Of course, you brushed your teeth this morning . . . We can help you bring out the natural beauty that you see there." In short, the purchase and use of cosmetics involve many psychological factors of personality.

### Three Kinds of Cosmetics

We can distinguish between three kinds of cosmetics. The first kind serves as a mask, cover, or disguise. It includes lipstick, rouge, and mascara. A second kind has to do primarily with health and care of the skin. Examples are cold creams, skin foods, and lotions. A third kind consists of perfumes and other products which appeal to the sense of smell.

### Cosmetics as Masks

The custom of staining the face is at least five or six thousand years old. The women of ancient Egypt tried thus to improve their appearance. Throughout recorded history, nearly all women everywhere have followed this custom. This is because it satisfies basic psychological needs. For instance, one of the main reasons for using cosmetics is that we can thus protect ourselves from the critical reactions of other people. We can pretend to be more attractive than we really are. Many of us, too, are self-conscious. With cosmetics we can disguise ourselves, as if seeking to hide from the world. "I do not like my face an awful lot. I'd like to change a feature here and there," said one of our respondents.

This form of self-protection started with Adam and Eve. The same defense mechanism is used by the child who puts his hands up in front of his face and imagines that he has disappeared. Modern women, when they apply cosmetics to beautify their features, exhibit a similar psychological tendency to mask their true selves. With them, however, the tendency is no longer a conscious one but a subconscious relic of primitive habits. It is no accident that some of the best-known cosmeticians, such as Max Factor and Elizabeth Arden, have had years of experience in making up actors and actresses.

Many women report that if they go out with no make-up on, they feel as if they were partly undressed—somewhat exposed, unprotected. The psychologist interprets this reaction as implying two conscious reasons for using cosmetics: the desire to avoid being too conspicuous, and the desire to maintain privacy. By diverting attention from our external ap-

Trying to achieve the modern aim of being unique or different.

pearance, we can simultaneously hide and develop our inner personality. This is why the average woman feels obliged to follow the example of the majority. If the majority apply more coloring, she must do the same lest she become too conspicuous by being among the minority. "All the girls had lipstick on. I would have felt out of place if I had not had it on. You don't want to be different from the others."—"I suppose I use make-up because everybody else does it."—"I think the main reason that everybody uses make-up is that, if some used it and others did not, those without it would look washed out beside the others. If everybody stopped using it, I would also." Those are some typical remarks made by women who were interviewed.

*Decoration*

Individuals are not expected, however, to follow slavishly all the specific techniques of the majority. In fact, nowadays the individual is supposed to approximate the ideal of the majority by adapting her methods of self-decoration to her personal needs. While not varying too much from the social group, she must try to achieve the modern aim of being in some way unique or different. People do not insist on complete uniformity. They do not care particularly how thin a lady's eyebrows are, for they react to her as a whole person. Indeed, to approximate the ideal appearance accepted by her own social group, she may need thinner eyebrows than her neighbor. Modern women do not try to change, but rather to emphasize, the individual characteristics of their personalities. This idea was stated repeatedly by our respondents: "You can't really rely on make-up to change your appearance. I just put it on to enhance what I've got. If you'd see me without it, you'd know why I use it." Such comments indicate understanding of the proper functions of cosmetics.

The psychologist points out that efforts of an elderly woman to use excessive make-up as a means of looking youthful may boomerang. The result may be that people will assume such a woman to be much older than she really is. Facial make-up should be regarded as part of the individual's complete personal adornment. Many women, because they are aware of this, now use different kinds of facial stain when they wear different costumes.

## Chemical Cosmetics

The chemical cosmetics are supposed to help us obtain a soft skin, a pure complexion, and a healthy appearance. Undoubtedly these are desirable qualities of personality. But what are some of the psychological reactions involved in the use of chemical cosmetics?

Even when a cream or other chemical solution is discomforting or displeasing, many people derive pleasure from applying it: "I like the process of preparing for a special occasion. Sometimes the occasion doesn't turn out so well, but I enjoy the preparation. Sometimes the preparation for it is better than the evening." How painstaking and complicated are some of the treatments used by modern women! And the more intricate the procedure, the more enjoyment does the beauty-seeking woman derive. One young lady explained: "I study the lines, and contours, and the shape of my face. The art of make-up is a complicated matter." The same reaction is found among men. Some men could shave themselves better than their barber shaves them, but they prefer the barber's ritual, including the hot and cold towels and the massage. The psychological explanation is this: From life experience, most people conclude that the best rewards result from the greatest effort and endurance. Furthermore, they tend to attribute magical secret powers to creams, unguentines, and lotions. They ask themselves, "Why would people take the trouble to manufacture, distribute, and use such products unless the desired beautifying effects were attainable?" Propaganda and skillful advertising have reinforced, and capitalized on, the simple age-old idea: The greater the effort, the better the results. A clever advertiser knows that it would be disastrous to advertise how simply and quickly his beauty products work.

Our doctor may tell us that the best thing for the skin is to wash it with soap and water. Do we accept his judgment immediately? Not at all, for how could simple products like water and soap have the same effect as those complicated magical creams and lotions? The vast majority of us are spellbound by the idea of secrets and of complex procedures. This is why intricate applications of cosmetics please us and lead us to anticipate miracles.

Cosmeticians use the term "beauty recipes," and quite properly. Whether applied to cooking or to cosmetics, the word recipe has the same psychological significance. "How to become beautiful" is an ancient slogan. Since primitive times, the search for effective secret potions and the use of mysterious formulas have persisted. How can we explain the individual's insistent demand for ingredients that are not known to others? A young woman, asked why she kept trying out all the new brands of cosmetics, replied: "Maybe some day I'll find something better than all the other girls."

But, if secrecy is so highly valued, why do women freely pass along to others their information about preferred beauty products? Perhaps they do this because of a desire to please others by imparting valuable advice to them. Such word-of-mouth advertising of beauty products creates the impression of sharing confidential information. The person allowed to share in the secret is doubly appreciative.

## Perfumes and Odors

A woman is flattered when someone recognizes her by her perfume. Such recognition means that the perfume is individual, fittingly associated with her personality. It means that she has purchased something distinctive that sets her apart from others and reflects good judgment. The psychological reason for using perfumes is not to get rid of body odor, but to substitute for it a gratifying and more pleasant odor that will attract the favorable attention of other people.

It is said that the sense of smell grows less keen as we mount the ladder of civilization and that, eventually, human beings will lose their olfactory power altogether. When that time comes, men may find it hard to understand how anyone could ever have detected the presence of food, such as cheese, without seeing it. In our day, however, we depend in great measure upon our sense of smell, with which certain subtle and complex psychological reactions are associated. In recalling a situation, we often remember first some peculiar odor associated with the memory. Thus, the odor of dampness or of rain may remind us of Paris or of some other city we have visited when the weather was rainy. In the same way, the odor of a perfume may remind us of a person who uses that perfume.

One of the main reasons for using cosmetics is to make ourselves appear glamorous, appealing, full of mystery. Love and romance are delicate matters. The advertiser of perfumes knows that to use very subtle references is the best way to associate anything with love and romance. This cannot be done by printing in large, bold letters, "This perfume is romantic." Likewise, moving pictures imply romantic sentiments through the complex personalities of the actors. This subtle association of moving pictures with romance explains why leading actresses are often used in advertisements of cosmetics. The actress's face reminds us of romantic ideals. Few people stop to think that without her whole lovable personality, all the face creams, lipsticks, powders, and perfumes in the world would not make her beautiful. Even in our sophisticated era, it is still true that a person is admired for what she is, not for what she looks like.

*Suggestions*

Insofar as the use of cosmetics is an indication of a systematic attempt toward self-improvement, it is desirable. If it becomes nothing but a façade, it is undesirable. Peace of mind, a clear plan for your life, satisfaction—these are all elements which show more clearly on your face than any amount of cream and powder no matter how skillfully applied. Real beauty comes from within. It can be enhanced if it is already present, it cannot be painted on if it is lacking.

Beware of advertising which makes exaggerated claims for cosmetics. Use common sense in applying cosmetics. Remember that there is no magic in secret or complicated formulas. Often, soap and water are the best things to use. Don't try to substitute external appearance for real growth in personality. There is no substitute.

Home, sweet home....

Philosophers and poets in all ages have glorified the virtues of home. What does home mean, however, to the sober realist? What does it mean to the woman who devotes most of her time to homemaking? To answer these questions, we completed a study of 4,500 American women. Of the women interviewed, 81 per cent declared that they obtained real satisfaction from housekeeping. Analyzing all the responses, we discovered that we could classify most American home-makers into three distinct types.

The first type is *the true housewife*. Her interests are monopolized by her home. The second type is *the career woman* (or potential career woman) who hates housework. The third type is *the balanced homemaker*. She does both housework and outside work, or is capable of doing both.

### The True Housewife Type

From the psychological point of view, housekeeping is this woman's dominating interest. She takes the utmost pride and satisfaction in maintaining a comfortable and well-run home for her family. Consciously or subconsciously, she feels that she is indispensable, and that no one else can take over her job. She has little, if any, *desire* for a position outside the home, and if she has one it is through the force of circumstances or necessity. Because human personality often expresses itself in our reactions toward everyday products, we can learn much about a woman's personality from her attitude toward refrigerators, dishwashing machines, and similar household appliances. The true housewife's reaction to appliances is somewhat mixed: She appreciates the advantages and help they offer, but is inclined to be critical or skeptical. She may even fear that they will render unnecessary the old-fashioned way of doing things that has always suited her.

In reply to a question regarding appliances, one such woman said: "Oh, I don't really need anything. That's up to the people who get up ideas. They always have something new. You can get a pressure cooker that cooks a chicken in five minutes, but is that healthy? The more you have, the more there is to go wrong, too. Of course, conveniences are nice, and nobody can really appreciate a washer who hasn't scrubbed her hands off on a washboard. But you take a wood stove—you can't beat a wood stove for a baker. It's the dry heat; gas heat is so damp. Well, the new things are quicker, anyway, even if they aren't quite as good."

Another woman's comment was: "I don't think there is any way to make housework easier for myself, because I don't believe that a machine can take the place of handwork. A machine cannot think, and you can't rely on it; it doesn't do as thorough a job as a person. Oh, it might work easier in some instances, but it can never replace a human being."

A third woman protested: "Do you really believe a machine gets the laundry clean? It is never as white and beautiful as when it is done by hand; it always comes out sort of grayish. Besides, it ruins the laundry. If you ask me whether the shorter life of the laundry pays in saving labor, I never looked upon it that way. It just hurts to see it go faster."

It is this reluctance to accept new devices that has to be recognized and overcome by manufacturers and advertisers, lest it lead to resentment and unreasonable fault-finding in regard to equipment. The number of women in this group has undoubtedly diminished in recent years, and will probably continue to do so, since new fields are now open to women. Many have come to realize that they will be better off if they are at least capable of holding down a job outside the home if necessity arises, and that modern equipment helps make this possible. Nevertheless, this group still predominates in the appliance market; we find that it represents 51 per cent of our total sample.

### The Career Woman (Or Would-Be Career Woman)

The term applied here is not meant to indicate that this woman is necessarily a job-holder. Many in this group have never actually worked, but they feel sure that they would be happier if they were not "imprisoned" in their homes, and they do not believe that primarily "a woman's place is in the home." They perform household duties under protest, inner if not open, and feel that in doing them they are wasting their energies and talents.

This state of mind is particularly significant for anyone who would sell appliances to such a woman, because her demands and expectations regarding them are likely to be unreasonable and unrealistic. What she really wants is to be able to press a button and, presto, find all the housework done. Her attitude is best exemplified in her own words, as spoken by a typical respondent of this class: "I find housekeeping is a horrible waste of time. If my youngsters were

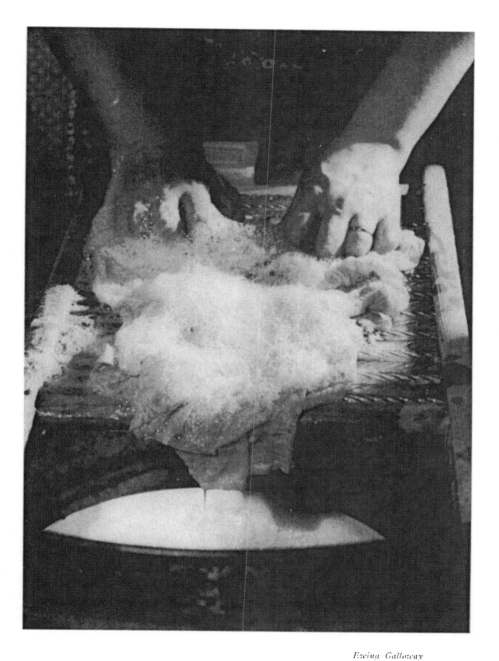

Laundering clothes the old way.

old enough, and I were free to leave the house, I could use my time to better advantage. If my family's meals and laundry could be taken care of by a competent person, I would be delighted to go out and get a job."

Another commented: "I want a mechanical maid. That's what I want—a robot. If they can make other things, they can make them, too."

Still another said: "I can tell you my ideas about housework in three words, I hate it. I've always hated it, and can't remember ever feeling any differently."

It is plain that the attitude of the career woman is not a very healthy one. The point to bear in mind regarding these women is that, while they buy modern appliances, they are not the ideal type of customer, and need a good deal of education in homemaking. In our national sample, these women comprise the smallest group: 11 per cent of the total.*

### The Balanced Homemaker

As the title implies, we have here a type that stands midway between the two extremes. This woman is the ideal type. She has an interest both in the world outside the home and in managing a well-run household. She has confidence in her ability to do and enjoy either or both, and hence is endowed with a well-balanced personality. If she is keeping house, she is apt to have some outside work, whether paid or voluntary, or she has held a job before turning exclusively to homemaking.

The balanced homemaker has an intelligent and realistic attitude toward mechanical appliances; she readily accepts the help they can give, but does not expect them to do the impossible. Obviously, then, the women in this group are the easiest to "sell" and are the manufacturer's best prospects.

* Of the responses in our survey, 7 per cent were unclassifiable.

Laundering clothes the new way.

In our national survey, they were found to comprise 31 per cent of the total.

This group is increasing in number, and there are several reasons. First, it is becoming more difficult to shift household tasks to servants, while at the same time a whole new generation of women is being educated to do work outside the home. Further, an increased desire for emancipation is evident. The attractions of modern living—magazines, books, radio, movies, sports—are incentives to acquire more free time.

All three types of homemakers, however, are influenced by the same basic psychological factors. Some of these factors apply to other animals, as well as to man. For instance, the desire for safety, for protection, sends some animals scampering for treeholes in which to hide from danger. Home is an anchorage amidst a stormy world, a place in which to store food and to avoid the hardships of weather, a fortress against enemies. This desire for protection, however, is of minor importance nowadays—that is, it is a factor that is taken for granted. A prospective house-buyer may evince some interest in protection against inclement weather, but most of his expectations are related to certain other psychological needs, particularly the need for a feeling of social security.

Young lovers dream about "a home of our own." Their conception of an ideal home is usually quite definite, although, in the course of necessary adjustment to reality, they may have to modify their expectations considerably. In the main, their ideal home reflects the need for security. It is a small, cute house, with a cozy fireplace, and a general snugness which suggests warmth. People who are about to marry feel especially the need of social security. They are embarking on an entirely uncharted and pleasantly danger-ous path. To have a place of their own provides them with a bit of earth that belongs to them, a refuge reserved for them in which they will be unmolested and free from fear of the threatening pitfalls of life. Any real-estate man will verify the fact that people want an attractive, "substantial-looking" house because they derive from such a home a feeling of security.

Social prestige is another factor in choosing a home. If clothes make the man, so do homes, and to an even greater degree. Comments such as, "He comes from a good home," or "This is a real home," indicate the great importance people attach to their homes. And with good reason. People need something to offset the natural weakness of the individual in a world of insecurity and danger. We all try to surround ourselves with protective shells. In our homes, we conceal ourselves and achieve privacy. Thus, our behavior in the privacy of our homes provides an excellent test of our personality. To find out what other people are like, we should watch them decorate a room, or we should visit them in their homes to observe how they have arranged their furniture and what colors they have chosen.

Social imitation also has great influence on homemaking. How often we see people living in surroundings that are in no way adapted to their practical needs! They imitate or cater to the tastes of others, perhaps in the arrangement of their furniture, or even in their choice of a neighborhood in which to settle down. Such people are afraid to be individuals, to follow their own desires. To be an independent individual requires courage, for it is much easier to accept ready-made customs. Modern people, however, guard against this temptation to imitate others slavishly.

Often social imitation can be traced to childhood experiences. For example, Mr. B—— always lived in huge apartments. Each room had to be exceptionally large. We traced this desire for extraordinary size to the fact that in his childhood he had had to live in narrow, cramped quarters. His whole existence was a "tight" one. Always he remembered this background and, as an adult, highly successful in his chosen career, he went to the other extreme. He felt happy only when in oversized rooms, obviously too big for him. And yet, in another case, the experience of an unhappy childhood had just the contrary effect. Mr. D——, a young executive, from a home where poverty was the order of the day, had slowly worked his way up to a point where he could easily afford a luxurious, or at least a very comfortable, home. Nevertheless, for many years he refused to live according to his newly acquired station in life, and he persisted in selecting apartments too small for his needs. Finally, he acceded to his

People are now paying more attention to efficiency in homemaking.

wife's idea that he should have a more pretentious home, in keeping with his social position. He purchased a new and costly house, but, brought up in a family which had considered any luxury wasteful or sinful, he almost suffered a nervous breakdown because of inner feelings of guilt and fear. He had not yet shaken off his sense of insecurity and his intense fear of waste.

But why does an attractive house seem to provide more security than a modest-looking one? Actually, property that looks expensive gives others the impression that people who own it are influential, successful, superior, strong. Among ancient tribes, the sturdiest house offered the best protection against enemies, and it was also attractive to the owner's fellow tribesmen. If a tribesman could build a strong hut, this showed that he himself was strong and skillful. He derived added protection, in that he no longer had to prove his superiority. In modern times, an expensive house does not necessarily offer more protection than a cheaper one, but it does add to one's prestige and thus increases the feeling of security. Our friends are impressed more by an elegant house than by a simple dwelling. Fortunately, people are now paying more attention to efficiency in homemaking than to social prestige. Strangely enough, the emphasis on practical efficiency has not impaired, but rather has improved, the beauty of the modern home. Thus, to build a more practical house, people began to use more glass and other useful materials. They planned the building to fit in with the surrounding landscape. They stopped thinking of indoors and outdoors as two separate worlds. The outdoor living room became a very important feature in connection with the modern house. Such developments reflect a feeling of real security. People no longer need so much of what Thorsten Veblen called "conspicuous consumption," that is, a scale or manner of living designed to impress others.

*Suggestions*

Try to be a balanced homemaker, avoiding both extremes of "the true housewife" type and "the career woman" type. Choose and adapt everything in your home to meet the needs of your personality. Instead of trying to impress neighbors or friends, make your home an efficient and esthetically satisfying place for the people who live in it.

# WHAT ARE YOU GOING TO HAVE ?
## (LIQUOR)

What are you going to have? Our host asks this question with a certain pride. He is proud of being able to offer his guest many different brands. Intoxicating drinks have been consumed for thousands of years, and have been under attack for an equally long period of time. Poets have praised alcohol, wise men have condemned it. Robert Burns wrote:

> "Leeze me on drink! It gies us mair
> Than either school or college;
> It kindles wit, it waukens lear,
> It pangs us fou' o' knowledge:
> Be't whisky-gill or penny wheep,
> Or any stronger potion,
> It never fails, on drinkin deep,
> To kittle up our notion,
> By night or day."

What is there about drink that makes it irresistible to some? Why has the custom of serving intoxicants endured so long? Undoubtedly, the initial effect of alcohol is to stimulate in a pleasant manner. The real reason for drinking, however, is not physiological but psychological. One middle-aged businessman testified: "I really hate the taste of whiskey. The taste is no better than medicine, but I honestly do like the glow you get after a drink or so. You seem to understand everybody better than before." Another person explained: "I guess the pleasure, or result, or whatever you want to call it, of drinking is to enable you to do things you can't do when you are sober."

## Drinking Removes Inhibitions

People today cannot obey all their momentary impulses, for they are subject to a high degree of inhibition. Our daily lives are controlled by ethics related to duty and discipline. Drinking is a form of rebellion against that discipline which religion and moralistic education have imposed on us. But the crust of civilization is relatively thin. It can be broken through easily. There is a constant tug-of-war between our sinful desires and the efforts of parents and of society to lead us away from temptation. Usually we do succeed in suppressing forbidden desires, but since this victory is not a very secure one, penalties are generally required to induce us to walk the straight and narrow path.

As youth matures, the struggle between impulse and moral code becomes more intense. Particularly during the period of sexual maturation, the natural passions tend to manifest themselves, despite all moral inhibitions. Nor is the influence of the custom of drinking altogether one-sided. It can affect young people in two opposing ways. It can give youth the courage needed to break through established codes, or it can strengthen the determination of abstemious individuals. Social pressure and prodding may stimulate the spirit of rebellion and encourage drinking habits. As one young fellow put it: "They got the girls up against me for not drinking. 'He's not a real man and that stuff.' They called me a sissy." The close connection between drinking and inhibitions is well indicated by the fact that people take pride in being able to hold their liquor. It is accepted as proof of one's being a "real man." One young man testified: "Well, I'll say this: If you can't get plastered and handle yourself like a gentleman, then you shouldn't get plastered." But, just as the heavy drinker feels proud of his potency and strength, so does the abstemious person feel righteous and self-confident. One person put it this way: "I've never been tight. In other words, I always come home under my own power." Another of our respondents declared: "I would hate to be known among my friends as a heavy drinker."

The struggle between guilt feelings and the desire to indulge is universal. Psychologists know that a person should be able to indulge in socially acceptable whims every once in a while without too great a feeling of guilt. He can apply strict rules of morality to every moment of behavior only at the price of excessive inhibitions which destroy his sense of freedom. He will benefit from occasionally indulging his desires, though, of course, such indulgence should not take the form of excessive drinking or other harmful acts.

### Are You a Connoisseur?

The social aspect of drinking is highly significant. Thus, people not well known to one another serve drinks to break down the social barriers which tend to keep them apart. Said one respondent: "I think it's nice to have a drink or two when people are in. . . . It really breaks the ice, and then everybody does it." The sociologists Thorsten Veblen and the Lynds have commented on the significance of social drinking, as follows:

"Drunkenness and the other pathological consequences of the free use of stimulants therefore tend in their turn to become honorific, as being a mark, at the second remove, of the superior status of those who are able to afford the indulgence. Infirmities induced by overindulgence are among some peoples freely recognized as manly attributes." *

"The speakeasies, like their now legal successors in Middletown, the 'taverns,' performed a dual function: as a physical place for meeting new people, and, psychologically, as an environment conducive to spontaneous human associations. The first explanation is more apt for the working class, since they do not have the money for entertaining at home or for elaborate entertainment outside the home. They lack the necessary home furnishings, telephones, etc. The business class has other means for making social contacts—lodges and clubs, for example, while the working group finds the taverns the only means open to them for meeting socially. . . . On the psychological side, most urban people, particularly the less aggressive personalities, need the facilitation of spontaneity in social intercourse which an institutionalized agency of informality provides. The speakeasy and the tavern, like bridge playing for the business class, help to institutionalize spontaneity. Here one sees a cityful of people, with little chance in their workaday lives to be directly personal in a spontaneous sense, finding out a way in their leisure to circumvent the strait-jacket set for them by their culture. One can talk or sit quietly in a tavern and have no feelings of self-consciousness." **

Our researches show that the label of the beverage has still another social meaning. Social prestige attaches to serving a well-known brand. People are less concerned about the taste and quality than they are about the class to which a brand belongs. We discovered that one of the first things people do, when buying any new brand of whiskey, is to ascertain to what category the brand belongs. Classification is not always

* Thorsten Veblen, *The Theory of the Leisure Class,* p. 70.
** Robert S. and Helen M. Lynd, *Middletown in Transition,* pp. 274–76.

a matter of price. Advertising and the shape and appearance of the bottle are frequently the decisive factors. For instance, consistent use of "high-quality" advertising to suggest luxury, and similar appeals, can permanently raise the social evaluation of a brand. A good example of this is "Four Roses" whiskey. It is not considered an expensive whiskey, but clever advertising has raised it to the same class as more costly brands.

The following comment reflects this factor of social prestige: "I don't honestly believe one advertisement as compared with another. Still it's a satisfaction to know I serve a good brand and, of course, maybe other people can taste a difference; and anyway, they do see the bottles." Public esteem for brands or types of liquor has been modified by moving pictures and literature. This factor should not be underestimated: "I think Scotch denotes a more experienced, sophisticated drinker. I got that idea from the fact that, in books, people are always ordering Scotch and soda, but no one ever orders rye. Also, in the movies, Scotch and soda is frequently specified, but never rye."

To have a well-stocked bar at home is a sign of prosperity. A bar in the basement is even more impressive, particularly if it closely resembles a real bar. Why do such things thrill people? One reason is that many of us enjoy a feeling of freedom from discipline or moral controls. We get this feeling of freedom when we participate in morally questionable activities in our homes. The popularity of gambling with pinball machines and roulette wheels can be attributed to the same psychological reactions. The person who takes part in minor sins in the privacy of his own home feels that he is safe from intrusion by outsiders who might express disapproval. He feels independent, and able to provide for his personal tastes and desires. Here's the way one man put it:

"I like to have several bottles at a time at home. I like to look at them. It gives me a rich feeling to know that I have so much in stock."

## Drinking as Escapism

In times of discouragement, when the problems of life seem insoluble, many people try to run away from the challenge. They seek a form of escape, which is in itself a kind of temporary solution of their problems. They hope that by drinking they will be more capable of facing the situation than when sober. Certain respondents expressed their attitudes as follows: "I drank to escape, because I was very unhappy at the time. I had very few friends, and I drank alone when they weren't around. I used to get tight alone, but as soon as that would happen I wouldn't be alone any more. I would go over to the first guy I saw and start talking to him." Again, "One's personality undergoes somewhat of a change under the influence of liquor. Things seem intensified. There are no inhibitions. You feel cleverer, you feel better about life and about your problems."

To many it seems all right to drink in company in order to break the ice or to escape from difficult problems. Most drinkers feel that it is not proper—some, that it is, in fact, wicked—to drink alone. "The time of drinking makes very little difference to me," said one person. "I feel a little wicked if I drink in the morning, but only because of what other people would say if they should see me." Evidently the person who drinks alone tends to think about what he is doing. He understands more or less clearly why he is drinking. In company, however, it is a different matter. He can rationalize and express himself boldly as if he were in a new social world. Most of us do not like to see women get drunk. Here again, we realize the real reasons why such women drink.

They demonstrate in their appearance and behavior the unpleasant features which we tend to ignore in men: "Where and how a man can drink, a woman can, too. Only if I have to see one drunk, I'd rather it would be a man."

### The Bartender—Knower of Souls

The bartender and, to some extent, the salesmen in a liquor store serve as father confessors and advisers. When we questioned bartenders, they would comment as follows: "Some come in here and say, 'Jesus, I feel terrible, fix me up,' and I'll say I'll give him a whiskey sour."—"Some man comes in and says he's tired, and another comes in and wants to commit suicide, and guys have come in who made 130,000 bucks that day and want to feel happy." These typical statements bear out our contention that people drink in order to find a solution to their problems.

As to distinguishing between different brands of liquor, most drinkers claim to be experts. But our experiments proved that the great majority are poor judges of quality. When we put expensive whiskey into cheap bottles, this misled the so-called "connoisseur." The same thing happened when cheap whiskey was put into expensive glasses. Experienced drinkers could not discriminate among different grades of whiskey. Actually, whiskey of poor quality and less alcoholic content was usually found to taste better. This is explained by the fact that high-grade liquor desensitizes the taste buds on the surface of the tongue so that the drinker finds it relatively tasteless.

When buying whiskey in a retail store, most people are in doubt as to the brand to choose. As long as they keep ordering their favorite brand, there is no difficulty, but if their pet brand is unavailable, they develop a feeling of insecurity. The salesman must then serve as a counselor: "A salesman can push almost anything. Customers simply beg to be told what to take."

One of the best ways to cure a drunkard is to discover and help him eradicate his psychological difficulties. He may be seeking to run away from his problems or he may be trying to get more courage to face his troubles. This explains why he accepts the bartender as his father confessor. The bartender is there to provide a source of escapism and courage. Unfortunately, excessive drinking is an inadequate, awkward, and stupid way of coping with the problems of life.

The shape and appearance of the bottle are decisive factors.

*Ewing Galloway*

*Suggestions*

Many attempts have been made to explain why man has been drinking intoxicating beverages for thousands of years. Perhaps the most common reason for drinking is the felt need of help in adjusting oneself to life problems. Drinking seems to give the individual a feeling of courage and superiority. Such people lack these qualities when sober, and realize their inadequacies. To combat habitual drunkenness, we must deal with basic psychological rather than moral principles. Thus, we must show people how to overcome the temptation to escape problems and realities. We must help them to achieve self-understanding and faith in their own capacities. We must help them to learn why they act as they do. Then they will be enabled to control, reject, or follow their real desires on the basis of knowledge, instead of being enslaved by ignorance and habit.

If you are ever tempted to drown your sorrows in drink, at least set a definite limit beyond which you will not go. In this way you will avoid guilt feelings and misgivings. If you feel that you cannot stick to a strict regimen, however, don't start. Instead, concentrate all your energies on solving the problems which are leading you to seek a means of escape. No matter how difficult life may seem, do something constructive about the situation and you will no longer have to depend upon artificial sources of courage.

# PART IV

## THE SOBER SIDE OF LIFE—HEALTH
## AND EFFICIENCY

Everybody wants to be healthy but most people think of health as a state of merely physical well-being, and they tend to ignore the fact that mind and body are inseparably intertwined. A highly nervous person who constantly gulps his food and thus develops an ulcer is inclined to blame the food he eats instead of his own psychological maladjustment. To increase our satisfaction and efficiency in everyday living, we should consider the psychological influences that affect both physical and mental health. What, for instance, does the psychologist say about our eating habits?

Physicians verify the fact that digestion is closely related to psychological health. Any experienced physician can cite numerous cases of patients who feel pains which seem to have no physical cause. Often such people are supersensitive individuals who center too much attention in themselves. This close interrelationship between attitudes and physical well-being implies that in order to keep our bodies in good condition, we need to understand the psychological influences which affect our health and efficiency. We need to analyze the sober side of life.

She spends much of her time for sake of health and efficiency.

# A PSYCHOLOGIST WATCHES YOU EAT

Do you feel bored when you eat alone in a restaurant? Well, you need feel that way no longer, if you will keep your eyes open and observe the people around you. Watch them carefully, and you will add psychological spice to your meals.

Even those of us who are not at all interested in science get a thrill from visiting a chemical laboratory or looking through a telescope at unknown worlds. But few of us realize the fact that marvelous things are always happening in which we play a part. Our everyday world is a huge laboratory, with human beings the subjects, and human behavior the problem to be studied.

Raise your eyes from your food, then, and look about you. Look toward that corner table. Note how that stout gentleman encloses his plate with both hands, as if he were afraid that the food might suddenly be snatched from him. Compare his table manners with those of that lean, straight fellow at the next table. To the latter, eating seems to be a necessary job that has to be finished in an orderly, systematic manner. Now look at the young lady at your left. She seems to be studying her plate as though it were an interesting landscape. Then observe her companion. He gives the impression of hating food, for he attacks it with ferocity and, when the tender steak yields at last to his weapons, his face glows with a gleam of victory.

What would a psychologist say about these people? According to modern psychology, everybody's personality expresses itself in many different ways. Whatever a man does —how he walks and talks, his gestures, the way he shakes hands with you—gives a psychologist important clues to understanding his character, attitudes, and emotions. To the trained observer, the eating habits of people have psychological significance. They are among the earliest habits we develop. Any mother of several children will confirm this, and will testify that each child has his own special way of eating. One little tot wants to be fed by Mother, while another refuses to eat unless he is allowed to hold his own spoon.

Eating habits persist. Once we have developed a habit of this kind, we are likely to adhere to it the rest of our lives. Such habits are seldom changed and, when change does occur, it can usually be shown that our whole personality has undergone radical modification.

Although eating habits supply clues to personality traits, they do not, of course, tell the whole story. The psychologist considers these habits in his analysis of personality, but he never relies on such observations exclusively for general conclusions. We should keep this limitation constantly in mind: Eating habits provide merely a few suggestive clues to certain traits of personality. Such clews are significant only if they are corroborated by many other characteristics.

All of us have our own mannerisms at table. Still, despite individual differences, a comparatively small number of personality types can be distinguished. The first of these is the possessive type.

## The Possessive Type of Eater

In his behavior pattern, the possessive type displays a sort of protective attitude. He treats a plateful of food as if it were a most valuable possession, to be defended against possible marauders. This attitude is shown in a variety of ways. A possessive diner may hold, and manipulate, knives and forks toward himself so that every movement resembles an encircling maneuver. He may even hold tight to his plate with one hand, as if fearful lest his food be taken away. When eating in a group, he may dart furtive glances at the food of his neighbors as if to make sure that they have not received larger portions than he.

The possessive eater tends to make his bites, forkfuls, and spoonfuls as large as possible. As a result, his soup will always overflow, and bits of food will drop back upon his plate or spill on his clothes. As we observe such a person, we wonder whether the memory of many hungry days is subconsciously driving him to store food in his stomach as quickly as possible, before hard times come again.

Many of our possessive eaters are hoarders of food. Just as their overloaded spoons reflect the desire to get more than they can eat with ease, so their general attitude toward food reflects the desire to possess more than enough for all their present requirements. What kind of personality would a psychologist expect to find behind these external manifestations? Would the attitude of a possessive eater toward food display itself in other life situations?

The answer is, yes, on the average. The possessive type of eater is, more often than not, very careful to hold on to all his possessions. He is probably inclined to be jealous, to envy others. He can never get enough of anything he desires. And basic to all these attitudes, looms a constant submerged fear of losing everything. Often, such a possessive attitude has its roots in a childhood lived in poverty. The possessive eater has had to earn things the hard way, and has had to struggle to defend his possessions.

## The Infantile Type of Eater

How frequently we have observed people at table who always take a long time between bites. If we watch closely, we shall see that their attitude toward food is a playful one. The implements—fork, knife, and spoon—are used like toys. The food is not brought directly to the mouth but is at first carefully manipulated, as in a game. Mashed potatoes become an imaginary mountain to be climbed; the sauce might represent a lake or an ocean; the spinach might be trees. With persons of this type, it is worth while to note how they arrange the food. They almost always turn the plate so that their favorite food is directly in front of them. Before eating, they hesitate a few moments while they re-arrange the contents of the plate. How the infantile type hate to have anyone else add sugar to their coffee or put ad-ditional food into their plates! Invariably, they insist on doing it for themselves, even though their instructions would be followed strictly. They reject any offer of help. It seems that they must add their individual touch to each dish. In a way, they act as though they were finishing at table the job started by the cook.

Most of the infantile eaters have similar attitudes toward other things in life. They are likely to display a playful at-titude toward serious matters. To a great extent, they carry into adult years the characteristics of childhood. They show immaturity when faced with difficult problems, and, instead of dealing with such problems in a specific, direct way, they evade the issues and seek detours or escapes.

At the same time, many such people are artistic and possess

good creative ability. They are individualists, often quite original in their thinking.

### The Ceremonial Type of Eater

The ceremonial eater insists on an orderly arrangement of all table accessories. Napkins, forks, and knives must be perfectly straight, and absolutely in their proper places. For them, everything connected with eating must be orderly and systematic. The meat is cut into small pieces. Foods on the plate must be rearranged in neat order. The various foods must never, never be mixed with one another. The ceremonial eater sits straight, not bending over his plate. After each bite, he always puts his knife back on the plate at a 90-degree angle. Never must the knife lean against the table. Ceremonial eaters have a horror of using improper implements—butter knife for meat, or meat knife for butter. Eating must take neither too long nor too short a time. It is a job that must be completed in the most efficient and orderly manner. The mouth is kept closed until the food has reached the proper height. The timing is much better than in the case of the possessive eater. And, unlike the possessive type, the ceremonial person abhors overindulgence.

Among ceremonial eaters, the traits displayed at the dining table are transferred to their other activities. They are orderly in their work. System and planned organization govern their everyday lives. They are likely to exhibit a certain amount of asceticism and abstemiousness, with rather rigid moral standards and a critical attitude toward others. If they are compelled to deviate much from their self-imposed rules and standards of conduct, they may suffer a breakdown of self-confidence and may lose utterly their feeling of security. Perhaps their pedantry can be attributed to an effort to compensate for excessive overindulgence in childhood or youth: having reformed, so to speak, these people tend to go to the other extreme, as if to prove to themselves that they have irrevocably mended their ways.

The three types of personality here discussed represent very broad classifications which, in reality, often overlap. In fact, each of us has a little of all three kinds of attitudes toward food. But one of these attitudes may predominate, in which case we can classify the individual accordingly. The problem is to strike a balance among the table manners and personality traits overemphasized by the possessive eater, the infantile eater, and the ceremonial eater.

FOOD FADS, FANCIES, AND FETISHES

From a psychological point of view, what we eat is just as significant as the way we eat it. How we develop our food habits is of little concern, so long as such habits involve only a few minor peculiarities. When, however, they lead to harmful dietary practices, they demand attention. What are *your* food fads, fancies, and fetishes?

Many food fancies stem from childhood experience. In childhood, most of us had little freedom to choose when, what, or how we would eat. Solicitous parents prescribed our meals, and usually insisted upon foods and beverages which were "good for you"—such as milk. But soda pop, hot dogs, and candy were reserved for special occasions, or as rewards for good behavior.

Maturity carries with it freedom from such control, and this release from discipline causes many people to acquire a dislike for milk and other foods that are "good for you" and a pronounced fancy for soda pop, hot dogs, and candy. It is still human nature to want most what we have been most denied. Seeking these forbidden satisfactions is one of the ways in which we try to throw off the restrictions of childhood and assert our independence. Consequently, certain foods come to be regarded as symbols of restraint, while others are accepted as symbols of freedom. Thus, Prohibition is said to have created habitual drinkers of many young people who thought that it was smart to break the law and assert themselves.

If you are inordinately fond of sweets and other "forbidden" delicacies, perhaps you, too, can trace such habits to childish fancy.

Countless peculiarities related to food may have similar beginnings. If children are left to their own devices, there are few concoctions that are too strange for them to try as secret expressions of their independence and daring. The same is true of many adults. We recall one respondent who likes marmalade on fish, and another who combines tea with coffee. These are the food fancies whereby they proclaim to the world the bold freedom of their maturity.

Although as adults we are free of parental regulations, a sense of wrongdoing persists at times if we violate the former injunctions of our parents. To assuage this guilt feeling, or to substitute a new authority for that of our parents, we may voluntarily accept all sorts of dietary restrictions.

According to where we turn for information and guidance, this can be the beginning of scientific food regulation, or it can be the beginning of faddism. Our food habits may be termed scientific if they have a logical basis. They are faddist if they depend upon uncritical obedience to common misconceptions or exaggerations.

Often there is a great deal of truth underlying a food fad. The fad of Fletcherism, for instance, which urged us to chew each mouthful of food twenty times, is based on the known fact that chewing helps digestion. Victor Heiser, the celebrated physician, has stated that thorough chewing is one of the foremost rules of health. But it becomes a fad when carried to unreasonable extremes.

Vegetarianism has been called a fad; yet, one of the main nutritional evils of our day is underconsumption of fresh fruits and vegetables. A vegetarian may properly be considered a faddist only if he gives wrong reasons for his beliefs, or carries them to a point where he may unbalance his diet and endanger his health.

## Fetishes in Food

A fetish is cousin to a fad, but is much more individual in nature. It is any material object, such as food, to which unnatural powers or significance may be ascribed.

For instance, primitive peoples believed that eating the heart of a lion would impart the courage of a lion, and that eating a rabbit would impart the timidity of a rabbit. These are examples of food fetishism—endowing simple articles of food with lifelike attributes of their sources.

### RED MEAT FOR HE-MEN?

It may seem far-fetched, but the man who insists on eating red meat for its he-man qualities is not far removed from such primitive beliefs—nor is the woman who will eat nothing but the daintiest of foods, for their "feminine" qualities. Notions such as these are fetishes unless a scientific or rational basis for them exists.

### FOODS LINKED TO EVENTS

Food fetishes may be of many different types. We recall a man who would not eat red beets. "I just don't like them," he explained, but later we discovered the *real* reason. Beets reminded him of an incident involving the shedding of blood. Another respondent refused ever to eat breakfast. Dis-

This he-man demands red meat.

cussion revealed that a violent family quarrel had once taken place at this meal. He omitted breakfast in a half-forgotten attempt to erase the episode from his mind.

If we write down some of our food dislikes, we may find, on careful thought, that they have little to do with taste. We may be associating foods with unpleasant experiences which are entirely irrelevant. Our dislikes may be fetishes.

### WHITE FOODS AND PURITY

Some of our fondest food preferences may be similarly suspect. For example, whiteness is commonly held to be a symbol of purity, both moral and physical. Hence, white foods, including bread and spaghetti, may owe much of their popularity to this ancient superstition. Of course, whiteness has little to do with food purity, and still less with moral rectitude. On the contrary, actually, in the case of grain products, it is an index of inferior nutritional value. Endowing white foods with the special virtues of cleanliness is a typical food fetish.

### SUBSTITUTING FOODS FOR PEOPLE

We can make fetishes of some foods because they remind us of a person or a thing we have liked or disliked. We may acquire a preference for a certain food merely because a person of whom we were very fond liked it, or because such a person served it to us. This sentiment may be so strong that giving it up would seem disloyal to a sacred memory.

Lonely people often fall victim to such fetishes. They may eat a particular food because of its associations with pleasant memories of people or places, or they may eat it to compensate to some extent for lack of love and companionship. We suspect that many people become too fat as a result of these fetishes.

Food odors of almost any kind may arouse pleasant or unpleasant associations with people or with places. The odor of cheese, and even that of milk, attracts some people and repels others. What passes for taste, in such instances, is really a fetish. These people associate certain foods with unpleasant or pleasant memories that, actually and practically, have nothing to do with food.

Fetishes are expressions of our individuality, and they are not significant unless they interfere with health, as when a craving for sweets leads to overweight. When our tastes take us along dangerous paths, however, it is time to investigate them. Discovering their true origin is a fascinating adventure, and is frequently all that is needed to correct a bad habit.

### Suggestions

Make an inventory of the undesirable tastes you would like to overcome, and the desirable ones you would like to cultivate. See how far back you can trace each like and dislike. Ask yourself frankly why you eat the foods you do eat. You may be surprised to discover how many of your food preferences are without rhyme or reason, and are actually rooted in fads, fancies, and fetishes which should be banished from your pattern of living.

Have a variety of foods so that there will always be something to look forward to. Don't eat as though eating were merely a conventional event, or as though it were an unavoidable obligation. Don't eat as though eating a great deal were the most important thing in life. Don't imitate an epicure or start complaining about the menu. Become enthusiastic about your meals. Try to begin with appetite and zest, eat until you feel you have had just enough, no more or no less, and then be sure to stop.

# your MIND can make you Constipated!

Each year the American people spend millions of dollars on laxatives. Constipation is a widespread affliction. It is nothing new in the history of mankind, for even the most primitive tribes found it necessary to seek effective remedies. Nor can it be attributed to a sedentary civilization, for no occupational group seems immune to the malady.

Modern physicians know that constipation may be caused, in some cases, by serious organic diseases. At any rate, chronic sufferers should consult competent physicians. In our research studies we discovered that many people ascribe this illness to emotional tensions. Here is what one person said:

"I worried all the time about making a living. Ever since that time, I've been constipated. Maybe I'm always constipated because I'm very nervous. And yet, I don't act like a nervous person. I don't move around all the time. I just feel tied up inside. I've felt this way ever since I can remember."

Is it really true that your mind can make you constipated? Many of us, when we have trouble on our minds, hesitate to assume responsibility for the situation. A convenient way of shifting responsibility is to look for some external cause of our troubles. Some people attribute their failures to lack of self-confidence or to laziness. They use these terms as if they were describing a mystic power over which they had no control. They seem to think that nobody should blame them for their lack of self-confidence or ambition.

## It's the Devil's Fault

People of the Middle Ages explained their ailments in much the same way. Each disease had its own special little devil inside the sick person's body. Sickness was caused by this inner devil, and often a good beating was administered to the patient to drive out the devil. Our modern victim of constipation relies upon a new kind of devil called "natural inclination." He says that he is inclined to become easily constipated. Like the devil of the Middle Ages, this modern devil explains nothing, but it relieves many a chronic sufferer of his obligation to do something about his ailment.

Each of us has tremendous power over the functions of the body. Modern medicine no longer accepts the idea that body and mind are entirely separate from each other. Physicians attest that numerous ailments once attributed to organic causes are actually caused by worry, fear, and other undesirable, and controllable, mental states. Body affects mind and mind affects body.

This should not surprise us. We see, on every hand, evidence that the mind has great influence on the body. When we are embarrassed, we blush; when we are afraid, we grow tense; when we are anxiously waiting, our hearts beat fast. None of these physical reactions is caused by organic disturbances. Embarrassment is a mental experience that affects our blood vessels; fearful thoughts tighten up our muscles; the psychological feeling of suspense affects the heart functions. And, as the great psychologist William James once remarked, these physical reactions seem to intensify our feelings of embarrassment, fear, or suspense.

The connection between mind and body is particularly significant in cases of constipation. This is because the organs involved—the stomach and the intestines—are among the most sensitive to mental disturbances. The ancients realized the peculiar sensitivity of the digestive and excretory systems. Thus, in the King James translation of the Bible, we read passages which reflect the ancient view that the bowels are the center of emotions:

"Joseph made haste, for his bowels did yearn upon his brother."

"Where are the soundings of thy bowels towards me?" There is some truth in this view. Our thoughts and feelings influence our bodily functions. They can either facilitate or impede digestion and elimination. And if we identify the mental experiences which retard normal functioning, we can try to avoid those causative experiences. We can strive to gain, instead, pleasant mental experiences which favor healthy functioning.

A young lady described her effort to control her body through mind as follows:

"I never allowed myself to be sick. It is usually people's own fault if they are sick. I am usually very strict with myself, because I have noticed that I could get away with murder. I haven't been sick very often. I depended very much on will power. I had stomach trouble for years, but I never considered that as being sick. I know now that it was not my stomach, but my mind."

### The Stomach—Power Plant of the Body

The stomach is the power plant of the body. In time of danger, the whole body is on the alert. The stomach then stops producing gastric juices, because most of the energy needed for digestion has to be available for prompt reaction to danger. With our attention concentrated upon the danger, we forget the normal functions of the body and, for the time being, such functions may be suspended. In some cases, however, the excitement prevents normal control, and diarrhea may result. The psychologist knows that diarrhea and constipation may constitute two physical consequences of the same urge to escape from danger.

How can we explain these two reactions—loss of control and excessive tension—to the same situation? In the human body there are two types of nerves: the *sympatheticus*, which act as stimulators; and the *parasympatheticus*, which act as inhibitors. The brain sends messages along these nerves to the muscles which control the organs of digestion and elimination. When we become aware of danger, the brain promptly mobilizes all the principal organs to prepare for action and thus disturbs the rhythmic movements of the intestines.

We must not think of danger as if it were merely physical. Worry, feelings of inadequacy, lack of self-confidence, and similar mental states are not very much different from the fear of physical danger. Any of these types of reaction may disturb our normal functions and, in this way, cause or aggravate constipation. Worrying about constipation helps to tighten up the muscles, and makes the original condition still worse. Constipation makes us worry more, and the increased worrying further affects the intestinal muscles. We are thus caught in a vicious cycle, a web of interaction.

## The Psychology of Retention

Constipation is not merely an involuntary clogging of the intestinal channels. Our case studies show that elimination is primarily a reflex process. But retention is usually subject to control by will power. We may be unable to compel certain organs to work, but we are able to keep them from working if we try to do so—until we lose *all* control, as in diarrhea. Ordinarily, our control of these organic functions is negative rather than positive.

## Feelings of Guilt and Shame

During our interviews, we discovered that many people blame themselves for having become constipated. Often they admit that improper diet and unhealthy routines of daily living caused their difficulties. Harsh discipline in childhood, as in cases of bedwetting, surrounded the whole subject of elimination with an aura of social disapproval and restraint. Psychological disturbances upset the normal rhythm and attitudes of children. Many cases of constipation reflect a vague mental state of rebellion and protest against harsh experiences of childhood. There is also another reason for the development of inhibitions and guilt feelings in adults. Processes of elimination are psychologically related to sexual tensions. Some adults with inhibitions related to sex transfer these inhibitions to the processes of elimination.

## Self-Medication

Most people do not consider constipation a major illness. Few of them consult their doctors about it. For this reason, the practice of self-medication has become most common in cases of constipation.

The variety of remedies available staggers the imagination. Many of them remind us of the ancient belief in magic. Often, self-medication indicates mistrust of the ability of physicians. Many people refuse to consult their doctor except in the event of very painful or serious symptoms of disease. The following remarks by a respondent illustrate this attitude:

"No. I never had a doctor or medicine or surgery. I believe in consulting a doctor only in vital cases, and otherwise handling the situation my own way. A natural way, mind you, like taking herbs and tea. I also don't believe in taking out the appendix or the tonsils, because they belong to the anatomy and should stay there."

Quite a few habitual users of laxatives seem to distrust doctors. Again and again such people assert that they "don't believe in doctors." With them, self-medication is really a substitute for the services of a physician.

### Suggestions

1. Remember that you cannot depend entirely on medicines to avert or relieve constipation. Medical remedies merely stimulate bodily reactions. Your mind must coöperate wholeheartedly.

2. Relax your body if you feel that you are too tense. Try to obtain a normal rhythm, a balance between relaxation and tenseness, in the organs of digestion and elimination.

3. Relax your mind, as well as your body. Worry causes muscular strain, which increases worry, which in turn increases muscular strain—a vicious cycle. Stop worrying!

4. Lead your body, instead of trying to drive it. Use indirect suggestion, instead of direct compulsion. Treat your bodily organs as if they were children to be guided, not stubborn animals to be driven. Like children, they will rebel against compulsion, but they will respond to suggestion.

# ARE YOU GETTING FAT ?

She had had a bad day at the office. The boss had criticized her work. When she reached home she was irritable, and a quarrel resulted. She felt miserable all the evening, and even worse the next day. She started to worry. Was she really slipping? Was her work getting poor? As the days passed, one thought led to another and, hardly realizing what was going on, she began to admit that her boss was right. Then she began to feel that she had really lost interest in her job. This process continued until she became almost a nervous wreck.

The case just described is typical of a common psychological process. As a matter of fact, it is the case history of Mrs. S——, a thirty-year-old office worker. At first, we were disposed to seek a rather complex explanation of her symptoms. Then we discovered the principal cause of her troubles. It was very simple. Mrs. S—— called it "the feeling of getting fat."

The physiological consequences of obesity are well known. We are concerned here with the psychological effects.

Getting fat is, as the expression implies, a process, in which we can distinguish three phases: the shock of discovery; the struggle for youth; and the period of rationalization.

## The Shock of Discovery

If we begin to get fat, usually we discover this fact in various ways. Perhaps summer is near at hand; unsuspecting, we try to put on our dress or suit which fitted us perfectly a year ago. After a few vain attempts, we realize suddenly that we have gained considerable weight since last year. Perhaps we see ourselves in the mirror from an unusual angle of vision, and we have to look twice to make sure that the image is ours, not that of a bulging stranger. Or we may experience the shock of discovery when a dear friend "makes no bones" of remarking on our bulky figure: "You are getting fat!"

Why does this little phrase hurt so much? Hearing it for the first time applied to ourselves, we feel as if we had received an actual physical blow. Why do we react so vehemently? Why are we not proud of ourselves, instead of feeling hurt? In certain other periods of history, obesity was greatly appreciated. Why is it out of style today? To explain our attitude as based upon changing popular tastes does not help to solve our problem, but merely brings up the question: Why has slimness become our beauty ideal?

The best answer, as we see it, lies in the fact that there are many more fat people among the elderly than among the young. Getting fat seems to imply that we are growing old. But why should old age be shameful? The Chinese look forward to it. Their whole philosophy of life favors old age, which is considered beautiful and worth while.

The attitude of western peoples toward old age is deeply rooted in our whole civilization. The economic and cultural structure of western society depends upon competition. While at school, we have to compete with other children. Most of our games are competitive. Success or failure, in almost every sphere of life, depends upon our ability to compete. In order to achieve victories, we have to be energetic and perfectly fit. Accordingly, people assume that youth is an important asset. Old age and, therefore, obesity imply lack of energy and of ability to win in competition against youth.

When we realize that we are putting on weight, usually we conclude that we are growing old, and our first reaction is to strive to regain youthful spirit and energy.

## The Struggle for Youth

Good health gives us a sense of security and of self-confidence. After our morning bath, we like to inspect our bodies in the mirror, stretch, and feel our muscles. We derive much satisfaction from these activities. The whole situation changes, however, as soon as we become aware that we have been putting on too much weight. We may then begin to lose our sense of security and self-confidence.

Very often, when a person begins to worry about obesity, he mentally forms a distorted image of his body. A fat man may picture his body as an exaggerated stomach to which the rest of his anatomy is attached. Invariably—though he will seldom admit it—he greatly magnifies the extent of his obesity.

There is a logical explanation for this tendency to distort the body image. The human body is a relatively heavy mass and, like every mass, contains several centers of gravity, one of which is the abdomen. These centers of gravity are also centers of psychological attraction. In other words, while normally we do not think about our bodies, we become sensitive to them as soon as changes take place in their centers of gravity. Excess fat constitutes a definite change in one center of gravity. Stout people worry about this change, and strive to correct their posture. They keep their bodies erect, in order to straighten the convex lines resulting from the enlarged abdomen.

What are the psychological consequences? Many such people, as they keep thinking about their appearance, begin to feel that others are watching them, too, and that others are discovering their unseemly appearance. They may develop a feeling of inferiority. Fortunately, they almost always seek means of compensation and reassurance. They may, for instance, start a reducing program. They may make heroic resolutions about diet and exercise. They may concentrate on the struggle to regain a slim figure, which is a symbol of youth. Some succeed in this ambition, others fail. Those who fail enter upon another phase of psychological reaction to obesity: the rationalization phase.

### Rationalization of Obesity

Human beings hate to admit defeat. Frequently, their first reaction is to assume a "sour grapes" attitude. Consider the stout person who has neither the courage nor the energy to regain his youthful appearance, and who therefore lets nature take its course. Does he readily admit his failings? Not at all. He seeks, and promptly finds, "good" reasons why obesity is not such a bad thing, after all; he lets it be known that he is a connoisseur who likes good food and a pleasant life. In time, he may even begin to look down on less portly individuals and refer to their "scrawny" appearance.

Our whole society has to some extent adopted this process of rationalization. A slim figure is considered ideal for youth, while obesity is tolerated, or even approved, in older people. In fact, a corpulent figure is often regarded as a sign of prosperity, connoting the ability to have all of whatever one wants —including food. It is supposed to endow one with authority and dignity. The superstition that fat people are truthworthy and invite confidence is nothing new. Shakespeare was aware of it when he said, through the character of Julius Caesar:

He likes good food and a pleasant life.

"Let me have men about me who are fat, sleek-headed men and such as sleep o' nights." Nowadays, stout women who have reached a certain age inspire trust and sympathy. There seems to be something protective, motherly, about them. Radio stars like Kate Smith lost no popularity from having a buxom figure. They reduced only for reasons of health.

As we have pointed out, fat people who suspect that others are constantly watching them become highly self-conscious. Such people may lose their spontaneity of expression and behavior. They tend to feel embarrassed and to develop inferiority complexes, especially if they are of an age when they are still trying to stay young. From our psychological experiments and analyses we have found that self-consciousness and feelings of inferiority may cause people to lose efficiency in their work and thus become subject to adverse criticism from others. Such criticism still further destroys efficiency and self-confidence. In this way, what started as merely imagined inferiority may actually lead to psychological disturbances, social maladjustment, and real inferiority.

What happens to those who fail in their efforts to reduce? Many of them develop a strong sense of guilt. To get rid of this feeling, they may try again to reduce. Unless they succeed this time, their sense of guilt increases. This explains why many stout people seem to be in a state of constant struggle within themselves, a struggle which leaves its mark on their nervous systems and, in extreme cases, may upset their entire emotional balance. We can understand, too, why those who give up the struggle to reduce transfer their defeatist attitude to other problems of modern living. Consider the case of Mrs. K——, a housewife of thirty-five. We analyzed the causes of her social maladjustment and discovered that she had formed an exaggerated idea of her obesity. She lacked the courage to begin the fight for a youthful appearance. She contrived all sorts of pretexts for "letting herself go"—excuses which she herself did not really accept. Her defeatist spirit showed itself in her attitude toward social problems and even toward her everyday work. She "gave up" not only in her dieting, but in every other activity that presented a serious problem or challenge. Eventually she regained enough self-confidence to make small successes in progress toward minor goals. But even these were important —she was on her way to a new psychological life.

## Suggestions

If you are overweight, hold fast to your self-confidence. Believe in yourself. Keep trying, for you have nothing to lose. So far as health is concerned, consult your physician. Adopt the golden mean: If you are getting on in years, don't be surprised that you have put on weight and don't try to keep up the appearance of extreme youth. If you want to reduce— under a physician's care, of course—set a reasonable goal, not one beyond your reach. Remember that obesity need have no adverse effect upon your work or social relations, so long as you keep your chin up and face reality with confidence.

You can get rid of fear, worry, and other undesirable psychological consequences of obesity if you keep busy with constructive activities. Goethe said that the one thing which made him feel proudest in his long lifetime was that he never became bored or pessimistic. There is always something new to learn, and each day should be filled with surprises, thrilling plans and experiences, new outlooks, and fresh starts.

# What bread means to you

Most of us eat bread every day as a matter of course. But have you ever taken part in a conversation about bread? If so, you probably realize that people have a great deal to say about their staff of life. We enjoyed such conversations with many people and discovered quite a few significant psychological facts.

For instance, all our respondents had pleasant memories of the bread of their childhood, that "good old-fashioned homemade bread." These are representative comments: "When I was a kid, my grandmother baked her own bread. That was the most soul-satisfying odor I ever smelled. She used to make Irish raisin bread, and when I taste Irish raisin bread today, I still can recapture the essence of that smell, and the delight of watching her fussing at the oven."—"I lived in a small town in Pennsylvania when I was a child. When we were small, my mother always baked her own bread. She used to bake twenty loaves on a Monday and put them in a special barrel. On Wednesday, all the bread was gone. She had nine children. I can still smell the wonderful bread as it came hot from the oven. It tasted better than anything I've had since."

In sharp contrast to these pleasant reminiscences about the bread of childhood are the flat descriptions of the bread which our respondents now have in their homes. To them bread has become a drab, unexciting food, of secondary importance, and taken for granted. "Bread," said one uninterested respondent, "is just something like salt, which you have to have occasionally to go with your food." Another sighed as she said: "It's hard to describe the difference in taste between home and store bread. It's the same difference as between spring water and city water. From a spring you can really taste the water. Here in the city it's just a liquid. When you eat modern white bread, it's just tasteless. You're just eating bread. . . ." So sharp is the contrast between fond memories of old-fashioned home-baked bread and contemporary reactions to the store bread of today that we are led to ask:

### Is Bread Still a Food People Crave?

A food is more than just something to chew and swallow. Food, in the real sense, makes the mouth water. To enjoy it, we must have appetite for it, and appetite depends on past experience. When we see a food we have once tasted and enjoyed, we feel an appetite for it, and we seek to relive the same pleasant experience.

Most of us have lost our former enthusiasm for bread. Can we ever regain such enthusiasm? Our researches lead us to doubt the value of current advertising which stresses the healthfulness of bread. Advertising would probably be much more effective if it helped consumers to recall how intensely they used to enjoy the old-fashioned home-baked loaf. Invariably our respondents referred to pleasant incidents connected with the eating of bread. The following nostalgic comment is typical:

{ 198 }

"I remember, in my childhood, my mother used to send me to the store to buy rye bread. I remember distinctly the lady picking it out from a whole mound of sour rye breads, putting it in a brown paper bag, and giving it to me. We lived three blocks from the store, and the whole way home, I kept my nose in the top of the paper bag. The fresh rye bread smelled so wonderful, and I used to come home with the tip of my nose all powdery from the end of the bread. Also, my mother used to laugh and say a little mouse had gotten at the bread, because I used to nibble at it on the way home, and sometimes I would have the whole heel eaten off by the time I got the bread home. Was that good!"

Here are similar reminiscences, all with that note of yearning for the past: "None of the bread can compare to what Mother used to make. What a wholesome fragrance! Of course, one remembers through rose-colored glasses, but it really was good! We used to have to wait around until it cooled off before we could eat it. Waiting aroused and built up a desire for that bread. When you got a piece of that, finally, it really was something!"—"Occasionally, my mother would give me a special treat of applesauce and sugar on rye bread, and I used to eat it very slowly, saving it carefully so that it would last through the whole story I was reading." —"When I'm hungry, the first thing I eat is bread and butter. It is very satisfying. Maybe it's a recapturing of youth. One of the first real foods you have is bread, and it is one of the first tastes you remember. Mothers always gave it to children. It was something they felt would not hurt them, no matter how much of it they ate."

Obviously, there are psychological reasons why people have changed their attitude toward the staff of life. The packaged loaf they buy at the chain store has not the advantage of association with Mother and enjoyable incidents of childhood. Nevertheless, most consumers still have their favorite brand or type of bread.

*Everybody Has a Bread Ideal*

None of our respondents hesitated to specify the qualities which they want in bread. Some felt that they had found these qualities in the bread they use. Others, less fortunate, still had a clear idea of what they want, and were rather hopeful about finding it. On the basis of numerous responses, we were able to determine the following qualities of the "ideal" loaf of bread: It should smell and taste good. It should be crisp. It should have body, substance, weight. It should never be soggy or doughy. It should stay fresh.

The people we consulted made use of vivid phrases to describe their ideal bread, as, for example: "I like bread that has some resistance when you bite into it. That's what I like in meat, too. Foods with resistance in them give me the feeling that I am more alive and a healthier animal." Again: "I look forward to this bread because it has an earthy feeling—almost alive. You feel you get close to the grain. It is not changed very much—almost as it comes from the field."

Whatever details the respondents gave, all agreed that the ideal bread is the one that tastes best. Whether or not it is also the most healthful bread, was considered of minor importance. The following comments sum up this point well: "I don't eat bread for health, so I don't care whether it has vitamins or not. If it tastes good and also has vitamins, so much the better. But if it tastes good and does not have vitamins, I would still eat it."—"No matter how many vitamins a bread had in it, I would not continue to use it unless it also tasted good." Evidently, bread advertisements which emphasize health rather than taste are based upon the wrong psychology! People have sense enough to know that their choice of a particular type of bread is not a life-and-death matter, so far as health is concerned. An opportunity to derive pleasure influences them much more than any logical analysis of their diet. One young woman said: "The Staff ads never said anything about the taste of their bread. They didn't tempt me to try it. Maybe that's why I haven't tried it yet, even though it sounded very interesting. After all, bread has to sound more than interesting. It can't only make me healthy. It has to taste good, too."

*The Breads of Nations*

The history of bread can be traced back for thousands of years. Many respondents were impressed by this long history, and mentioned it spontaneously. "Bread," said one woman, with much interest, "is one food you can trace all the way through history. One of the things found in the ruins of Pompeii was a petrified loaf of bread, right in an oven. Also, bread was dug up in some Egyptian tombs, showing that it was used as far back as 3000 B.C."

People all over the globe, of almost every race and nationality, eat some form of bread, no matter how strange their other manners and customs may be. "It's amazing!" exclaimed one respondent. "Everybody all over the world eats bread. It must be good if it's so widespread."

There are innumerable literary allusions to bread, proverbs that show the important role of bread in people's lives: "Cast your bread upon the water. . . ." "Give us this day our daily bread. . . ." "Bread is the staff of life. . . ." "Keep him at least three paces distant who hates bread, music, and the laugh of a child. . . ."

Superstitions reflect the way bread is anchored in human customs. Seamen fear to turn a loaf of bread upside down, as this is supposed to mean that a ship will be sunk. "The man who wastes bread will live to want," is another superstition. Another odd one is that a loaf of bread thrown into the sea calms the waves. Also, sailors put a loaf of bread at the base of a ship's mast as a forecast of prosperity and safe return. Misconceptions have developed, too, about the medicinal virtues of bread; it is frequently used as a poultice or healing agent.

Our interviews show that there are marked regional and national differences in bread preferences. People become accustomed to the bread of a particular locality, and when moving to a new region or traveling across the country, they often find it difficult to get the bread they want. Some have even insisted on taking their favorite bread with them or having it sent from home. "When my maid goes on her vacation upstate," explained one woman interviewed, "she takes several loaves of pumpernickel with her. You can get that kind only here in New York, and she says food doesn't taste good without it." Other respondents expressed similar views: "All summer I don't eat bread. They don't have the right kind at the hotel, so I'd rather do without bread. Up in Maine, you can't get the kind of bread I like."—"In Wyoming we met a man from the East. He begged us to mail him some good White Mountain bread. He couldn't get it in the West, and he said he had missed it terribly since he had moved out there."

These differences are even more pronounced between nations. Each person thinks the bread of his own country the best. Almost every country has a distinctive bread, as can be seen from the fact that we call types of bread by the names of countries, for example: French bread, Italian bread, Swedish crisp, Russian pumpernickel. To quote one of our respondents: "When I was in Sweden, I got quite used to Swedish bread. That was the only bread they ate. You couldn't get them to eat anything else, and I even missed it when we left." It is noteworthy that America has no national bread. Many of our respondents regretted the fact that there is no American bread with the distinctive character of a national or regional product. They would like a bread which could be identified with all of America, with American life.

### Don't Waste Bread

Many people consider it sinful to throw bread away. As one woman put it: "I never throw bread out. When it is too stale to eat, I make bread crumbs from it. I think of what a crust of it would mean to starving people. After all, it is a basic food." Such attitudes have given rise to many superstitions about wasting bread—like these: "I never throw out bread. They say it is bad luck." "Never throw bread out. Burn it." Some people are so fearful of wasting bread that they would rather do without it altogether: "I know I could never finish a whole loaf and I hate to throw it away, so I buy rolls or crackers instead."

### Good Enough to Be Eaten Alone

We seldom eat bread without other foods, and we have definite preferences as to the types of bread to eat in combination with certain foods. In our interviews, we collected such interesting comments as the following: "Some things I like better on white bread, and some better on rye. On white bread I like cream cheese and olives, and things like that. I like the more delicately flavored meats, like Virginia ham, on white bread. Rye bread has a more definite flavor of its own than white bread, and so it drowns out the indefinite flavor of delicate things. On rye bread I like things with a strong taste, such as meats, heavy cheeses, and the like."—"I connect different beverages with different types of bread. With white bread I think of milk, particularly white bread with butter and jelly. With rye bread and cheese I associate beer. . . ." Furthermore, some foods stimulate a greater desire for bread than others do. Here's what one man said: "Rye bread goes best with strong cheeses. Ordinarily I don't eat it, but if there's Roquefort cheese in the house, then I eat a whole loaf." And one girl reported: "I love white bread with jams and jellies. If there's white bread and jelly on the table, I'm a gone goose."

Incidentally, people tend to eat more bread when dining in restaurants than they do at home. They attribute this to the larger selection of bread offered in restaurants, where they enjoy being able to choose. This makes them pay attention to the bread, as contrasted with their indifference to it at

This traveling oven turns out 4,000 loaves of bread an hour.

*Ewing Galloway*

home. They grow tired of eating the same bread day after day, but they often find it impracticable to satisfy their desire for variety. In small families, to supply a variety of bread would mean that some of it would go to waste.

## Made by Bakers, Not by Mechanics

Modern sanitary industrial baking facilities have had a quite unexpected psychological effect on most consumers. Our respondents almost invariably complained that the modern super-efficiency of large bakeries has resulted in colorless, tasteless, and uninteresting bread. They insisted that bread made in small bakeries or in homes benefits from greater personal care and the use of higher-quality ingredients. Such misconceptions prejudice consumers against "factory" bread, as witness comments like the following: "When I think of a bread factory, I think the producing probably takes place on a sort of assembly line, just like in a car factory. I do not like to think of bread being made that way. Somehow it seems to lack the personal touch. A food should be made with individual care."—"Sure, the conditions are 100 per cent clean in bread factories. The bread is even cleaned of taste. They don't put such good ingredients in any more, as people used to when they baked at home."

At the same time, our respondents acknowledge the advantages of "factory-made" bread. They realize that it relieves them of a time-consuming task. They appreciate the fact that such bread is always the same, whereas homemade bread varies in quality. Furthermore, quite a few of them consider the factories cleaner and more sanitary than the small bakeries or even home kitchens. For many, these appeals outweigh any objectionable qualities. One busy housewife remarked, with feeling, on the time element: "I have no time to bake bread any more. It takes the better part of the day to put it in the pans, have it rise twice, put it in the oven, and so on." Another stressed the uniform quality of "factory" bread: "At home, you never can tell if bread will turn out well, but it's always uniform from the factory."

## Consumers Want a Way to Test Bread

In choosing bread, people use several sense organs. They lift it, squeeze it, smell it. One respondent said, very definitely: "I can tell which bread is fresh, and which stale, by touching and smelling it. It's more difficult these days, though, when all the breads are wrapped in wax paper." People get used to the weights of different kinds of bread, and try to estimate whether or not the weight of a loaf is up to their expectations. Some women test the bread in every conceivable way before buying; they want to be perfectly sure of satisfaction. Frequently, people pick up several loaves and read the wrappers in search of additional information about the product. A wrapper that stresses the merits of the bread and invites the reader to test its quality for herself seems most reassuring.

## The Ingredients

Most consumers know about the "fortified" breads, with added vitamins. "They do put something in bread lately. Some kind of thing they add to the flour. . . . They put it in to make people work better and faster and have more pep," remarked one purchaser. But people get vitamins in so many products nowadays that they pay little attention to the statement that vitamins have been added to bread. Besides, they are not very clear as to what vitamins will do for them, and many feel that the amount of vitamins in bread is so small as to be insignificant. The alert consumer is skeptical about advertisements that stress vitamins.

Few of our respondents stressed the relation between vitamins and health. Nearly all of them, however, considered bread a symbol of strength. Eating a great deal of bread was formerly accepted as evidence of power, virility, manliness. "My brother can eat a whole loaf of bread at a time," said one young man. "I've seen him do it. He's a husky fellow." Other comments also implied this idea of strength and energy: "When we were kids, no matter how large the bread was, we always cut it around the loaf. We liked to eat a great big piece like that."—"My nicest recollection about bread is when I was a kid. I used to eat tremendous slices of bread, with butter spread on them, as I sat in a big chair and read fairy stories." The alert advertiser tries to associate the vitamins in bread with the widespread idea that bread means health and strength.

A good many consumers eat less bread because they believe it to be fattening. Men and women alike attribute this effect to the starch in bread. One woman remarked: "If I wanted to reduce, bread would be the first thing I would cut out. It is so starchy." And a young man explained: "My dad was always against starchy foods. He doesn't let us eat much bread. He thinks vegetables are better for us than fattening foods." If bakers are to counteract this idea that bread causes obesity, they will have to do more than simply deny the allegation. They will have to provide convincing proof, and publicize it in language which the average reader can understand. Actually, when bread is plentiful, many of us would enjoy eating more of it, and that is the time when the bread industry should start a campaign to get rid of current misconceptions and inhibitions of consumers.

All our respondents had some knowledge about the ingredients of bread. The housewives among them had either baked bread or watched others baking it. Our Pure Food

An alert advertiser associates vitamins in bread with health
and strength.

Laws and government inspection reassure the consumer that
bread contains no injurious ingredients. Yet, there is a popular suspicion that commercial baking companies observe
only the minimum legal standards, and use synthetic products or substitutes in order to keep down the cost of production. A typical comment voicing this suspicion was this:
"I think that the ingredients in manufactured store bread
are probably pure. After all, they have to live up to their
claims and government standards. But I think they probably
use powdered eggs and things like that to save money."
People are reassured if the manufacturer states that "genu-
ine" ingredients, such as fresh milk and eggs, have been used
in his bread. Some of our respondents were impressed by
the claim that wheat is healthful. "I like the idea of wheat
so much," said one woman enthusiastically. "Somehow there

} 208 {

is something wholesome and healthy in the thought of it. As a kid, I used to feed the chickens with wheat grains and I used to eat some of them myself. Sometimes we kids would roast wheat grains and eat them. They were sure good. I still like seeded rolls that have the grains of wheat stuck to them."

Consumers seem to consider rye and whole-wheat breads more healthful than white bread. These kinds are thought to have less starch and to be less fattening. People believe, too, that whole-wheat bread is much richer in vitamins. One person put it this way: "White bread is not good for you. You can squeeze a piece of fresh white bread, and moisture will come out of it. Bread so moist and doughy is indigestible." Many expressed vivid ideas about what happens to white bread during the process of digestion, as in these comments: "White bread just rolls up into a ball in your stomach, like when you roll it between your fingers. It must be indigestible, and so I prefer dark breads."—"You know what happens when you drop a piece of white bread into soup, it bulges out all soft and pasty. I imagine that's how it gets in your stomach, when the stomach fluids get at it." Accurate information should help to dispel these misconceptions about white bread.

*Suggestions*

Bread is not really the staff of life. In many countries it is actually a secondary food, for it is not of itself an adequate source of nourishment. However, you can learn to appreciate and enjoy such products in their proper place and function.

When buying bread, consider factors of health, as well as taste. Get rid of emotional over-evaluation of bread, and erroneous ideas that store bread is inferior and that starch or other ingredients are injurious. Finally, unless you have a legitimate reason for eating less bread, choose the kinds you like best and eat as much as you think is good for you.

Old-fashioned homemade bread varies in quality.

# The psychology of buying

Mr. Brown bought a new suit. Everybody knew it at once, not because the suit looked new, but mainly because Brown was showing it off to the world. He wanted to be admired. But more than anything else, he wanted to be reassured. No matter how much faith he had in the store which sold him the suit, buying it was an adventure full of risk. For, in our society the purchase of a relatively costly product requires the conquest of doubt and indecision. The consumer must dispel not only doubts about the reliability of merchants, but also doubts about his own needs and choices. Did Mr. Brown really need the suit he bought? Did he select the right one? Did he get the best value for his money? Such are the considerations that point to the psychological problems of every consumer.

Skill in buying has a profound influence on our everyday living. We generalize about security and happiness, but our ideals mean little unless we can obtain concrete practical evidence of security and happiness. Successful living consists of tangible little successes, as well as intangible or emotional satisfactions. The individual feels successful if he can purchase what he needs—if he has a nice new car of his own to admire, if he can watch a comfortable house of his own being built from blueprint to final form.

Although material possessions cannot satisfy us completely, the surest sign of unhappiness is the lack of things to enjoy. See how a new dress, a new toy, even a new crayon, any kind of valued possession, buoys up the spirit of a child and gives him a feeling of satisfaction. Understanding his need of things to enjoy, a child frequently counts his possessions in the same way in which King Midas counted his riches. Little Mary loves to exhibit all her dolls. With a sweep of her hands, she dramatically demonstrates her wealth—"Look at all my pretty dolls!"

What is the psychology behind our attitudes toward buying? And why are material goods so important in everyday living?

*Possessions Expand Our Personality*

In many countries, family descent to a great extent determined the individual's standing in his community. Descendants of the nobility were usually granted special recognition and privileges. In countries such as Germany, Spain, and Italy, for hundreds of years, possession of a title carried with it honor and prestige. This practice spread to some Latin American countries. In the United States of America there are no titles of nobility. Even here, however, some of our citizens substitute for nobility the claim to descent from early settlers, from fighters of the Revolution, or from Anglo-Saxon pioneers.

Since the vast majority of Americans cannot resort to these substitutes for noble descent, they make use of a more modern source of distinction: the trade-mark of the products they own. They may choose by trade-mark almost anything they wear, from head to foot, and almost anything they use in their daily activities. Matters have come to such a pass that it may soon be customary to describe an individual's personality not by referring to him as one who is timid or self-conscious or characterized by any other traits, but rather, for example, as one who wears an Adam hat, drives a Plymouth car, drinks PM whiskey, and wears Arrow ties and shirts. The individual's pride in these things is based on the prestige derived from financial success. Ownership of a Buick implies more wealth than ownership of a Ford. To people who respect economic achievement, a home address on Park Avenue in New York City means a great deal more than one on Third Avenue.

The popularity of numerous widely advertised products can be attributed to the prestige attached to them. Inherent quality and value are often secondary considerations. Advertising helps to establish a product as a symbol of success. Even in buying a toothbrush, we may be guided by claims that certain distinguished people use a particular type or brand. Some products are prized merely because the prices are relatively high and only the more prosperous use them. They are substitutes for claims to nobility and for pride in one's family tree. As for products that are low in price, to develop our sense of prestige in these cases we look for special qualities that seem to express our individuality. Our surveys have disclosed several qualities or values which make our possessions serve as mirrors or extensions of our personality. One such quality is newness.

## The Quality of Newness

Most people feel very insecure about colors and styles. Men depend on their wives and sweethearts to help them select articles of clothing. Not infrequently they rely upon women for decisions as to pattern and style.

A haberdasher thus describes men's buying habits: "In 98 per cent of the cases, what is bought depends on what the woman says. The man keeps asking, 'How do you like it?' If she says 'No,' the man does not take it. The men are all 'suckers.' They always come with their wives and with their sweethearts. I had a case like that only yesterday, where a young fellow comes in. He picks out a pair of socks. He says he will have to ask his lady whether she likes it. He doesn't have a mind of his own. If a man comes alone, then you have a chance to sell him, unless you don't have the article. When he comes with a woman, it is a hard job to sell him. If the men are alone, they decide very quickly."

Most people like new things. In fact, buying is often an excellent way to get out of a rut. One of our respondents testified: "Whenever business is very bad, and I feel really discouraged, I go down and buy myself a new hat or a new pair of shoes, or whatever it may be. It is not really important what I buy. Just the feeling that I can buy something new lifts me up, in a way, and I feel much better afterwards. The whole of life looks brighter to me." This person is not unique. Everyone can recall childhood incidents which confirm such influence on his personality. When is a boy prouder than when he can buy what he wants and pay for it with his own earned money?

New products provide a special thrill. We don't have to be keen observers to discover that one of our friends has just bought a new hat. We notice at once his unusual behavior. He will probably be most careful as to where he puts his hat; or he may hold his head at an angle as if he were afraid of losing his new possession.

The desire for new possessions seems particularly effective in inducing people to buy unnecessary clothing. Thus, a highly successful business executive reported that he bought

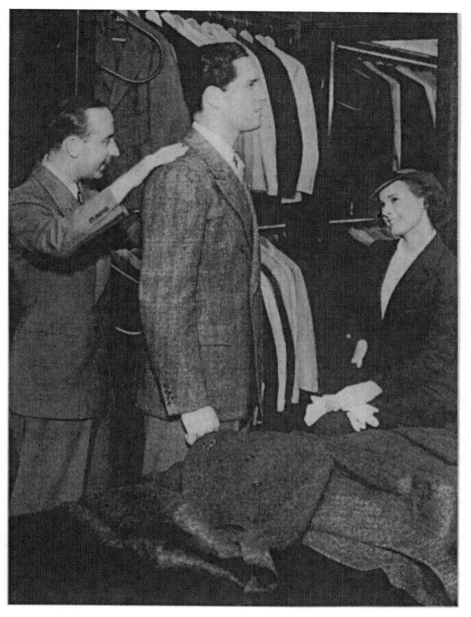

"What is bought depends on what the woman says."

a new hat every month. Among our respondents, such practices were not unusual. Many of them bought new outfits whenever they entered upon a new phase of their careers, such as getting married, changing their jobs, traveling to distant places. We can easily understand the significance of new clothing in some instances—a veteran returning home, or a woman becoming a nun. In such cases, new clothes become a symbol of the desire to get a fresh start, to start life anew.

*Weight Versus Delicacy*

Two apparently contradictory qualities of products profoundly affect our buying habits. One is weight or solidity, a value which can be traced back to primitive hunters, who prized heavy game and feared the power of larger animals. The other is delicacy or fragility, also a value handed down from ancient times by tribal chiefs who demanded artistic products for decorative purposes.

Modern consumers are impressed by the weight of merchandise. "It gives me a good feeling of owning something substantial if the shaver weighs a lot," said one respondent, who uses an electric shaver. "I like the feel of a sturdy little machine in my hand." His is a typical reaction. Men are generally influenced more than women by the weight of products such as fountain pens, typewriters, automobiles, and mechanical gadgets for the home. One businessman was so fond of solid, heavy possessions that he kept a bottle of mercury always on his desk, just as a trinket.

Large products have much the same effect as heavy ones. Some people enjoy immensely the prospect of eating a very large steak. Others like to wear oversized hats. In the same category as large steaks and oversized hats are big cigars, long bars of bath soap, ample powder boxes, tall bottles of perfume, and even sizeable flapjacks. Like the hunter of ancient times who felt secure from hunger after capturing a large animal, modern consumers gain the feeling of power, safety, and prestige from possessions that are impressive in weight or size.

Delicacy and fragility reflect an esthetic or even an effeminate taste, which can also be traced back to the earliest ages of mankind. These qualities are just the opposite of solidity and massive dimensions. Another factor in esthetic appreciation has to do with the uniqueness of a product. Advertisers appeal with great success to the ego of the consumer by advertising that their product, though manufactured by the millions, is designed by a famous artist. If we are really intelligent consumers, they imply, we shall appreciate the rare skill that designed so beautiful a product. This subtle compliment to the consumer's judgment often arouses in the purchaser a vanity that prevents accurate appraisal of the real worth of merchandise. Consumers need to understand the psychological influence of superficial factors such as weight, dimensions, and claims to uniqueness, for these are frequently minor considerations, so far as getting their money's worth is concerned.

## Smoothness

"Smooth as a baby's skin." This is a significant phrase to the psychologist, for it reflects the dependence of consumers on their sense of touch. People seem to have more faith in their tactile than in their visual sense. Soap, glass, silk, aluminum, highly polished wood, and similar products appeal to the sense of touch. Consumers get a thrill out of the pleasant sensation of smoothness.

One school of psychologists explains the powerful influence of touch as a variation of sexual gratification. A good

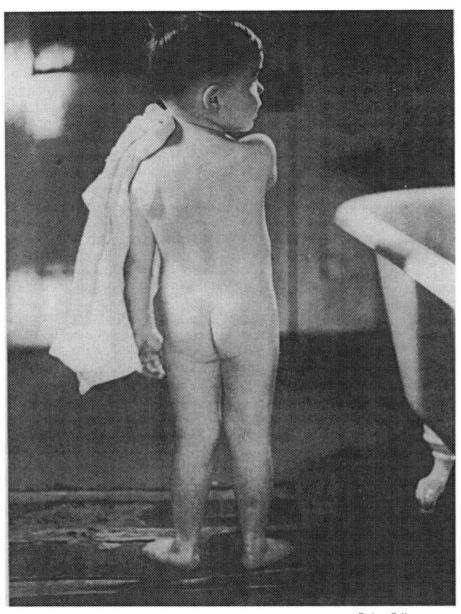

"Smooth as a baby's skin."

many psychoanalysts consider the reaction to smoothness a minor form of sex experience. Touching the skin provides a pleasant tingling sensation and makes us feel more fully alive. Perhaps this is why a person in great fear reacts sometimes by embracing himself or stroking his skin, as if to reassure himself that he is "all there." He seems to mobilize all his resources to "pull himself together," a term that accurately describes such a person's state of mind.

Many of us are skeptical consumers who, like children, wish to touch objects before making a choice. In fact, we are much too careless about touching things, as can be seen from the deplorably high rate of accidents caused by the handling of dangerous implements such as guns, bombs, and firecrackers.

## Suggestions

When you go shopping, distinguish between superficial factors, such as weight, size, uniqueness, and smoothness, on the one hand, and valid practical criteria on the other. Ask yourself what are the fundamental reasons for your choosing a product. Trace the origins of your preferences for a particular color or taste, or for other nonessential qualities of many products. Are you buying a fur coat to compensate for a feeling of inferiority, or is your choice based on careful consideration of the best investment for your money? The intelligent consumer makes sure that his purchase represents, not a protest against the drabness of life or some erroneous association with past experiences, but rather an objective appraisal of his needs and of the utility of the merchandise he selects.

If you form the habit of critical judgment concerning the values of merchandise, as distinct from superficial qualities, why not apply the same scientific attitude toward your selection of intangible things, such as ideals, friends, and books? That would help you to get along better with other people, to develop more definite goals, and to live a most meaningful, healthful, and enjoyable life.

Ewing Galloway

Buying has a profound influence on our everyday living.

# How to be happy while cooking

Cooking should be a pleasant and well-liked part of household duties. The woman who hates cooking and considers it a necessary evil can be sure that the fault lies in her own attitude. Cooking does not have to be a depressing chore. It is the way we look at our work which makes it either a creative, easy, and at times even thrilling job, or a drab, dull, deadening routine. Whether it shall be one or the other depends on us.

"But I hate to cook," protested one woman whom we consulted. Undoubtedly she thought so. Nevertheless, we have never met a normal woman who, "deep down," really did not like cooking. Those who profess an aversion to the culinary art usually do so because of one or more of the following factors: (1) They cannot cook well. (2) They do not appreciate the importance of cooking. (3) They dislike some of the chores associated with cooking, such as washing dishes. (4) They cook for unappreciative people. (5) They resent the people for whom they cook. None of these things, however, reflects upon cooking itself. Given the proper encouragement and knowledge, almost any woman will become a good cook if she wants to, and most women do want to be skillful in their household tasks. Some psychologists have even claimed that interest in cooking is based upon the instinctive nature of women. "Let me make a confession," said an eminently successful business woman at an afternoon tea. "I get a bigger thrill out of serving that cake which I baked with my own hands than out of any so-called 'big deals' I've ever put across."

Perhaps this pride in culinary ability can be explained by the fact that cooking is really only a form of feeding. Every normal woman has the desire to nurse, feed, and protect. Cooking is a modern expression of this primitive urge of the mother animal. Nor is the preparation of food an exclusive privilege of the human race. Birds and many other animals chew and prepare food before feeding it to their young. Some animals use the sun and other natural means to process their food. When a modern young lady gets married, she usually takes over this role of "feeding-mother."

Even the most sophisticated husband is proud of the fact that his wife is a good cook. There is truth in the old adage that the best way to a man's heart is through his stomach. How unfortunate it is that the average young American housewife cannot cook so well as Mother and Grandmother cooked thirty or forty years ago!

*Self-Assurance*

Of the women whom we interviewed about their attitude toward cooking, some liked to cook and others hated it. Our interviews disclosed some of the psychological causes of their attitudes, and suggested methods for increasing their interest and skill in cooking.

Skillful cooking provides self-assurance. Doing anything well gives us satisfaction. If we draw well, we shall like to draw. If we do a great deal of drawing, we shall learn to like it still more. The same is true of cooking. If we do not know how to cook, we cannot enjoy it. The better we cook, the better we shall like it and, vice versa, the more we like it, the more often we shall cook. Of course, there are some women who know much about cooking, but rarely use their skill. If, however, they do not use their skill to the fullest extent, they will not get the full pleasure out of cooking. Indeed, eventually they may lose some of the skill that they possess.

It is important to realize that pleasure from cooking depends on skill. This relationship between enjoyment and ability may influence one's whole personality. Most women need self-assurance much more than men do. Men have more opportunities to develop this trait. They have jobs and numerous interests outside the home, whereas women have fewer such opportunities. To be a good mother and a good wife, however, is one way to gain self-assurance and a balanced personality.

If we do not cook well, we must try to gain self-assurance from being successful in other tasks, but the satisfying role of "feeding-mother" can never be completely replaced. Further, dislike of cooking may lead to a dislike of all housekeeping and, eventually, to an unsatisfactory home. A negative attitude toward cooking should therefore never be accepted as inevitable, for any woman can become interested in the subject. Those who take helpful courses in school, or who study systematically at home, soon discover that they enjoy trying out some of their newly acquired knowledge.

Novice cooks complain that cook books do not present enough details or practical hints for the beginner. Most of them say they were once very ambitious and wanted to become experts. They purchased cook books and tried some of the recipes, but they were never quite sure about minor details of the advice given. For this reason, they failed to obtain anticipated results. Easily discouraged, many gave up studying after having managed to learn only enough to prepare a merely digestible meal. Analyzing the contents of numerous cook books, we discover that most of them neglect to encourage beginners to keep trying, despite initial failures. We wish the authors of such books would tell their readers the most common errors made in the use of each recipe. Food advertisers, too, should consider the effects of possible failure of housewives to get expected results from advertised products. Although the cook may not blame the product, but only her own lack of ability, she may nevertheless become discouraged and stop using the ingredients advertised.

## Pride in Results

One of the most frequent complaints of housewives is that, after they have spent hours preparing a cake, it disappears in no time. This feeling of having worked in vain is not at all justified. In whatever work we may do, we enjoy best the kind of effort which produces visible or tangible results. We like work which brings forth praise and recognition from our friends, employers, or others. Actually, a woman who cooks well produces the most useful and lasting results. The mother who says, "It gives me great satisfaction that my child has grown up by eating food prepared by me," appreciates the practical results of her efforts.

## Pleasure of Approbation

Few of us can do our best work for any length of time without being shown some attention or appreciation. Any intelligent employer realizes that. One reason why some women dislike cooking is that too often their work is merely taken for granted. Thus, a housewife complained: "When the food is all right, they never say a word, but if a thing does not turn out as well as it should, even if only once, they immediately find their voices."

Just as a worker in a plant or an office soon loses interest in his job if his welfare is being ignored, so the housewife will consider cooking a boring, routine matter if her work is not praised. A husband who complains about his wife's poor cooking would do well to investigate whether or not he himself is largely to blame. Perhaps inconsiderate husbands get the quality of cooking they really deserve.

### Ingredients

A good carpenter may be a complete failure as a locksmith. He may have the required aptitude, but may dislike working with iron. Some young housewives cannot endure touching raw meat or cleaning a chicken. Many do not like to handle mushy ingredients. Others consider dough rather messy to work with. The sense of touch plays a major part in cooking.

### "I Like to Cook but I Hate to Wash the Dishes"

Often women reject certain foods, and never include them in the family diet, simply because preparing such foods requires the use of many pots and dishes. No wonder considerations of health and taste are then of no avail. Actually, the young housewife who follows modern recipes can do her cooking with a minimum of equipment.

### "It Takes Too Long"

This is another excuse frequently given by women who do not like to cook. As one of our respondents put it: "I tried a new recipe, but I did not realize that it would take me all afternoon." This excuse is itself inexcusable, for anyone can

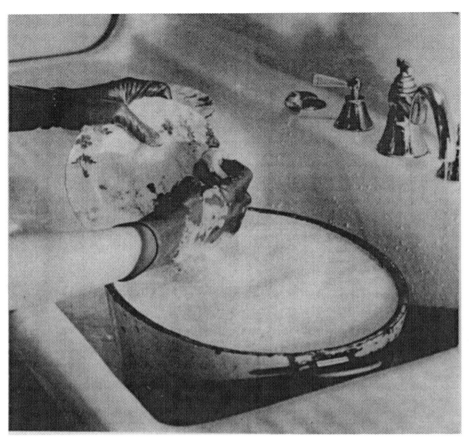

Washing dishes the old way.

learn to plan her daily schedule in accordance with the time available for cooking. Often, the time needed for preparing a meal can be reduced considerably by a "production plan." To prepare such a plan in a systematic way is always worth while.

### Cooking Is a Modern Scientific Occupation

Some housewives regard cooking as a task beneath their dignity or their station in life. They assert that their husbands would much rather see them do intellectual work or have them enjoy life otherwise than by spending all their time in the kitchen. This attitude is partly attributable to advertisements of canned foods and of other ready-to-serve foods. We do not suggest that women spend all their time in their kitchens. Nor do we imply that frozen or canned foods should be avoided. But we do insist that a modern housewife can be a good cook and still have plenty of time for other interests.

Cooking is a task worthy of the well-educated woman. Any woman who studies the problems of nutrition and the principles of scientific feeding realizes that such household duties require intelligence and considerable training. Modern cooking is not a job to be looked down upon. Knowledge of biology and of medicine is most helpful. Women who dislike cooking should reëxamine their attitudes toward other occupations, as well. They will discover that, compared with other fields requiring skill and years of training, the preparation of food is a highly respectable occupation.

## The Kitchen as a Modern Laboratory and Management Center

In many cases, the kitchen is the exclusive domain of women. Men work in offices or in similar places designed to meet the requirements of their occupations. Most women, unless they go out to work, use the kitchen as their headquarters. In too many instances, however, the kitchen has not been designed and equipped in the best way for the tasks of modern housekeeping. The typical kitchen is a relic of old-fashioned methods of work.

A modern laboratory is never full of steam or odors, nor should our kitchens be subject to such disadvantages. Fans, ventilators, and deodorizers are simple devices to install in the old-fashioned kitchen. Modern recipes are chiefly of a

Washing dishes the new way.

type that permits odorless cooking. Why not have a few bar chairs around, so that most of the work can be done while we are sitting down? There is nothing fanciful in having a few books on a shelf; and the need of a radio in the kitchen is almost self-evident nowadays.

## The Happy Bride as a Good Cook

The young bride who cannot cook well feels guilty about it. This drawback disturbs her. She would like to be perfect. Not knowing how to cook gives her a feeling of inadequacy and inferiority. It may often result in an attempt on her part to discover faults in her husband, in order that a balance may be established. Since it is not difficult to discover his faults, a dangerous basis for mutual fault-finding is thus established.

Men want to be sure they will be looked after as well when they are married as they have been before; to a certain extent, a wife takes over the role of mother. Men believe that good cooks are potentially good mothers. Every man wants his wife to be a good mother, for this is a basic purpose of marriage. A wife who cooks well shows that she does not take marriage lightly, but that she has prepared herself for her duties. She has brought something useful with her into the new home, and even in the most beautiful romance, each partner tends to assess what the other brings to the marriage. Knowledge and skill of this kind are definitely important assets.

Even the most self-assured Don Juan feels rather insecure when he gets married. The happy bride who is a good cook can help him to compensate for this feeling of insecurity. Being able to cook is closely related to being reliable, evidence that she knows her business, which, at this stage of life, is being a housewife. Most young husbands, moreover, are financially unsettled. They are worried about their budgets. Marrying a woman who knows how to cook well means a better chance of having fairly good meals on a small budget. Then, too, a good cook has a positive attitude toward her new job as a housewife. She does not regard housework as an unpleasant chore, nor does she think she has given up a brilliant career for a drab existence as a wife. Her husband feels reassured in knowing that she is happy as his wife and does not consider this role beneath her dignity. And just as a woman is proud to boast to her friends that her husband is an executive, so he is proud to tell his friends, or still better to prove, that she is a good cook.

Most men are vain creatures. To be served with poorly prepared meals is something they take as a personal insult. Note how indignant they become in a restaurant when the food is not tasty: "You don't think *I* am going to eat *this!*" The young housewife should not be misled by the outwardly indulgent attitude of her still romantic husband. He may say "Don't mind, " but his pride has been hurt. In fact, the discovery that he has married an inefficient housekeeper is a man's first disillusionment in his marriage. He feels cheated, for he had assumed that he was marrying a perfect individual. Now he fears that, as time goes on, other flaws may show themselves in his partner. Besides, he feels that he has a job of teaching on his hands—that, in a way, she has become a liability, and is not self-sufficient. The modern husband does not want a weak, dainty, helpless girl, but a self-reliant comrade. He wants to be sure that his wife will be able to face life with him. Finally, every young husband feels insecure in his social role. He needs social recognition. If he knows that his wife can entertain guests efficiently, he feels more secure. He wants to be sure he can invite friends, without having to warn his wife too far in advance, and still have fairly decent "pot luck."

*Suggestions*

Put a bulletin board on the wall of your kitchen. It will help you to centralize the manifold operations of your modern household. Buy a filing cabinet in which you can keep all the important folders of information on accounts, tradesmen, and stores. File your recipes so that they will be ready for use at all times. Don't make your kitchen the stepchild of all rooms, but give it the attention it deserves as the center of household management. Remember that cooking is an essential job for every woman, because it is necessary for her complete satisfaction. You can be happy while cooking. Learn to cook well. Develop self-assurance, and face discouragements courageously. Your health and the health of your family will be permanent records of your achievements. Organize your kitchen work. Use modern recipes, so that you will have fewer dishes to wash. Develop a production plan. Do all these things, and you will soon like to cook. As your skill grows, so will your pleasure increase. Bit by bit, you will acquire your kitchen degree.

A kitchen should be a modern laboratory and management center.

Voting in a referendum. Our task is to build democracy.

# PART V

## A TASK FOR THE SOCIAL ENGINEER

The crucial problem facing our people today is that of building a more democratic society upon the foundations of the past. Social scientists, educators, and other civic leaders have tried to teach the people the ways of democracy, but have not as yet achieved satisfactory results. The person who would logically benefit most from their efforts to make him a better citizen prefers not to be educated—he chooses entertainment, escape, and diversions instead.

Meanwhile, psychologists ponder the question, Why do radio "soap operas," true-story magazines, and comic strips arouse the intense interest of the public, while serious books, pamphlets, editorials, and speeches stimulate only the most casual interest? The answer is simple: The social scientist has been using the wrong approach and the wrong techniques. Consequently, he has merely helped the people to form the habit of paying superficial lip service to democracy. His verbal generalizations are a far cry from the realities—the challenges and everyday situations—of modern living. He has failed to use the "selling" techniques which should be used to impel people to live democratically, just as these techniques have been employed successfully to induce the masses to purchase nationally advertised merchandise.

To make a success of American democracy, we need to understand and apply effective techniques of social engineering.

## The Basis of Democracy

If we think of democracy as a way of everyday living, not as a set of abstract ideals, we can understand why the building of a democratic nation depends upon the practical and intelligent application of psychological principles. In a democracy, the people must make the critical decisions and govern themselves. If they are immature, neurotic, unhappy, or insecure, their democracy cannot possibly work satisfactorily, and it will do no good to preach about the remote goals of democratic government.

What is the use of propagandizing for desirable ideals if we go no further than that? We know how futile general statements would be in teaching people to be healthy, unless we also showed them, for instance, how to form better dietary habits. And yet, in teaching democracy, we still rely on verbalisms only. This cannot be effective. Reliance on preaching about the values of coöperation is useless and unscientific. If people are uncoöperative, the first step for the social scientist to take, if he really wants to improve their attitudes, is to gather facts. He should ascertain why people coöperate, or fail to coöperate, in their activities of everyday living. Then, after completing his psychological diagnosis, he will be in a position to suggest therapeutic procedures. A psychiatrist does not assume that he can cure a patient by merely explaining that the latter has an inferiority complex and should try to get rid of it. The expert recommends effective remedial experiences. So, too, in a democratic society, we cannot teach coöperation by telling people that they are uncoöperative and that they should try to coöperate in civic activities. We must do much more than that. We have to center our attention on very specific concrete tasks which each individual can accomplish, and we must use available scientific knowledge to build democratic attitudes and habits.

Thus, the psychologist has adequate knowledge as to the causes of the aggression which impedes democratic coöperation. He knows how to help individuals to get rid of feelings of frustration. The treatment of overanxious, neurotic patients is well established in psychotherapy. Insight into the basic motives underlying human behavior is essential for the development of tolerance—an essential trait in democracy—and psychologists can apply psychological techniques to achieve such insight. They understand the illogical thought processes that cause group antagonisms, and they are familiar with the psychological effects of demagogic propaganda. The scientific knowledge is available—but it must be *used* to influence millions of people through instruments of mass communication, such as advertising, radio programs, moving pictures, newspapers, and periodicals. For mass education in democratic living, we can no longer depend chiefly upon slow, inadequate, old-fashioned methods of teaching which emphasize glorified ideals that influence only a handful of people. We must use modern media of propaganda and publicity—the whole gamut of instruments of communication—that will influence the millions.

In our country today, we are confronted with the following situation: Advertisers, radio script writers, and editors know and use the correct techniques for reaching the minds of people. They are confused, however, as to the content they should put into their messages in order to help people become more democratic and coöperative—the task of democratic engineering. At the same time, they are forced to use more and more *intangible* appeals in dealing with intelligent audiences. Progressive educators, on the other hand, *know* what kind of influence they want to achieve, but they tend to use ineffective methods, for they generally *fail to utilize* the psychological techniques applied by advertisers.

### Social Scientists as Social Engineers

Fortunately, social scientists and social psychologists are being called upon by commerce and industry to lend their scientific training to the investigation of diverse practical problems. Their tasks range from finding out why subscribers did not renew their subscriptions to a periodical, to analyzing the psychology of smoking. These commercial assignments give the social scientist a unique opportunity and a compelling responsibility to be more than an academician who sells his thinking to advertisers. His research studies, quite apart from their commercial purposes, can contribute mightily to the progress of democratic living; they provide data needed for understanding the attitudes, motives, and behavior of large groups of the population. By acquiring such data, the social scientist becomes, in the truest sense, a social engineer. If he is trusted by merchants to tell them the best way of inducing consumers to purchase a particular make of automobile, or to help increase the popular appeal of a radio program, then, surely, he can also be trusted to assist in the social engineering of democracy. He can at least provide indispensable scientific information.

In preliminary research, including about one hundred base studies and the use of several hundred questionnaires, we tried to gain insight into the psychological needs of individuals as related to education for democracy. We asked the question: How can we help Mr. Brown become a better citizen with the aid of modern means of communication? The main theme of our investigation centered in the extent of the individual's satisfaction or dissatisfaction with the social order in the United States. Our purpose was to diagnose his maladjustment to society, as to both kind and degree, in order to clear the way for remedial treatment. Our study justified the following tentative conclusions:

Social scientists should use radio to reach the minds of people.

In their first responses, most of our citizens seem convinced that America is the best country in the world, and they appear to be well adjusted and contented. But, when we peel off this outer crust of docility, we discover that these people do not really believe what they say. They are frustrated. Three aspects of frustration can be discerned: (1) a feeling of political impotence (Three-fourths of all respondents declared that they could not exert any influence in this country); (2) a feeling that there is a wrong order of things in the nation ("Only crooks get ahead"); and (3) a feeling of futility and disbelief in progress ("It will never change").

These frustrations, as is the case with all frustration, lead to aggression. Curiously, aggression is directed against the government. People refer to the government as "they," as if speaking of some medieval devils. These people have a

CPSIA information can be obtained at www.ICGtesting.com
Printed in the USA
LVOW072142191012

303642LV00020B/154/P

9 781163 173923